APPROACH (ALMOST) EVERY BUSINESS PROBLEM WITH A.I

Himanshu Sinha
Approach (Almost) Every Business Problem with A.I
The Ultimate Playbook for AI Adoption and Business Transformation

All rights reserved
Copyright © 2025 by **Himanshu Sinha**

No part of this publication may be reproduced, distributed, or transmitted in any form or by any means, including photocopying, recording, or other electronic or mechanical methods, without the prior written permission of the publisher, except in the case of brief quotations embodied in critical reviews and certain other noncommercial uses permitted by copyright law.

Published by Spines Publishing Platform
ISBN: 979-8-89691-563-8

APPROACH (ALMOST) EVERY BUSINESS PROBLEM WITH A.I

The Ultimate Playbook for AI Adoption and Business Transformation

HIMANSHU SINHA

Contents

	Acknowledgments	vii
	Preface	ix
1.	Generative AI's Impact on Business Transformation	1
2.	Preparing for AI Adoption — Building a Future-Ready Organization	9
3.	Practical Guide to AI Adoption for Enterprise Leaders	59
4.	Essential Generative AI Terms Every Leader Must Know	79
5.	Transitioning from Machine Learning to Generative AI	103
6.	AI in Action — Proven Use Cases Driving Business Success	117
7.	AI and Cybersecurity — A Resilient Digital Future	171
8.	The Future of Generative AI — Emerging Trends and Opportunities	195
9.	Final Thoughts — Leading the AI Revolution	223
10.	Bibliography	231

Acknowledgments

This book would not have been possible without the unwavering support, encouragement, and inspiration from those around me.

First and foremost, my deepest gratitude goes to my wife **Vishakha** whose patience, and love gave me the time and energy to pursue this endeavor. Thank you for allowing me the space to immerse myself in writing, even when it meant sacrificing family moments. Your support has been my cornerstone.

To my numerous **colleagues & ex-colleagues**,

Ana-Maria Badulescu, Bryan Smoak, Dave Berman, Harish Kakde, Rajat Swaroop, Tim Segall

Thank you for the knowledge, insights, and lessons you've shared over the years. Each one of you has contributed to my growth and shaped my understanding. Working alongside you has been both an honor and a privilege.

This book is dedicated to all of you—my family, my professional mentors, and my friends. You've not only been my support system but also the driving force behind this work. Thank you for being part of my journey.

Preface

Before you dive in, there are a few things you should know about this book—it's not your traditional textbook.

It's a practical guide designed for both seasoned technology leaders and beginners wondering to step into the world of Generative AI.

Here, theory meets practice. Each chapter not only introduces key AI concepts but also provides real-world use cases and Python implementations you can apply immediately. Whether you're driving enterprise-level AI adoption, managing data science workflows, or exploring AI for the first time, this book has something for you.

We start with foundational AI concepts, progress to actionable frameworks, and dive into hands-on examples and industry-specific scenarios. You'll also gain insights into emerging trends, preparing you for the rapidly evolving AI landscape.

This book is your roadmap for leveraging AI to drive measurable impact. By the end, you'll be equipped with the tools and confidence to lead AI-driven change in your organization.

If you find a pirated copy, please contact me directly so that I can take action.

1

Generative AI's Impact on Business Transformation

"Businesses that are slow to adopt AI risk falling behind their competition, while those who embrace it will redefine their industries."

Sundar Pichai

The Tipping Point: Why Generative AI Matters Now

A McKinsey report reveals that advancements in generative AI have accelerated automation timelines by a decade. It now predicts 50% of 2023 work activities could be automated by 2045, compared to the previous estimate of 2053, highlighting AI's transformative impact on the future of work.

We are standing on the precipice of a transformative era—one where machines don't just compute or classify but create. **Generative AI** has shifted the narrative of artificial intelligence from automation to imagination, empowering businesses to generate entirely new solutions, ideas, and strategies. And here's the kicker: **it's happening faster than anyone anticipated.**

Organizations that act with urgency to adopt Generative AI are gaining a competitive edge, while those hesitating risk being left behind. Consider this: **90% of business leaders believe AI will transform their industry, but only 20% feel their organizations are ready to adopt it.** The gap between readiness and action is where opportunities—and threats—reside.

A Rapidly Changing Landscape

The urgency to embrace Generative AI is not just a buzzword; it's a reality driven by market momentum:

- **ChatGPT's Record-Breaking Adoption:**OpenAI's ChatGPT reached **1 million users in just 5 days**—a feat that took Facebook nearly 10 months. This adoption rate underscores the hunger for AI solutions.
- **AI's Economic Potential:**According to PwC, AI could contribute up to **$15.7 trillion** to the global economy by 2030. Early adopters will take the lion's share of this growth.
- **Market Leaders Taking the Leap:**Companies like Microsoft, Google, and Adobe are embedding Generative AI into their core offerings, redefining what customers expect from digital experiences.

In this fast-moving environment, the message is clear: act now, or risk irrelevance.

Generative AI: What Makes It Revolutionary?

Traditional AI models have long excelled at identifying patterns, predicting outcomes, and automating workflows. But **Generative AI** takes this to the next level by enabling machines to create content, generate insights, and even solve complex problems autonomously. It doesn't just follow rules—it writes them.

What Sets Generative AI Apart

1. **Creation Over Automation**: Traditional AI automates; Generative AI innovates. For example, instead of categorizing products, it can design a new product lineup based on consumer trends.
2. **Contextual Understanding**: Generative AI models like GPT-4 and DALL·E can interpret complex contexts

to generate tailored outputs—be it drafting personalized emails or creating on-brand visual assets.

3. **Scalability**: These systems are not constrained by scale. From creating content to optimizing supply chains, Generative AI can handle millions of tasks simultaneously, learning and improving in real time.

- Are your current business strategies leveraging AI as a reactive tool, or are you prepared to use it as a proactive creator of value?

Urgency Drives Success: The Risk of Waiting

Adopting Generative AI is no longer a strategic advantage—it's becoming table stakes. Organizations waiting for the "perfect moment" risk losing their edge. A delay in adoption could result in:

- **Revenue Loss**: Competitors leveraging AI can launch products faster, personalize customer experiences, and optimize costs, leaving late adopters scrambling to catch up.
- **Talent Drain**: AI talent gravitates toward innovative organizations. A lack of urgency in AI adoption can result in losing top tech and leadership talent.
- **Customer Expectations**: With AI shaping industries like retail, healthcare, and finance, customers increasingly expect personalized, AI-driven interactions.

The Business Case for Generative AI

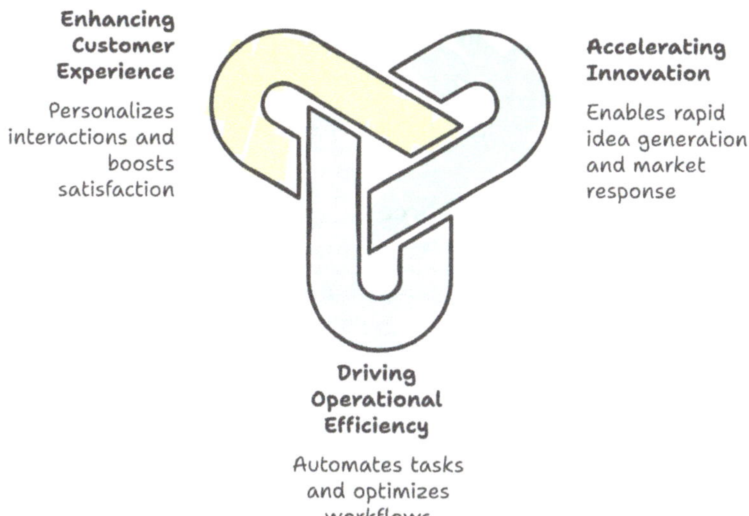

1. **Accelerating Innovation**

Generative AI enables businesses to innovate faster by automating ideation and prototyping processes. Consider a company using AI to design personalized product catalogs or generate marketing campaigns tailored to individual customer preferences.

2. **Driving Operational Efficiency**

From drafting reports to analyzing complex datasets, Generative AI automates repetitive tasks, freeing teams to focus on strategic priorities. Companies using AI-powered code generation tools report up to **40% faster development cycles.**

3. **Enhancing Customer Experience**

In today's hyper-personalized world, customers expect tailored interactions. Generative AI delivers this at scale by analyzing preferences and generating responses that resonate deeply.

Real-World Impact: Industries Embracing Generative AI

1. **Retail and E-Commerce**
   - **Example:**Amazon uses AI to generate personalized shopping experiences. With predictive analytics, it suggests items customers didn't know they needed, driving higher conversions.
   - **Urgency:**With retail giants rapidly adopting Generative AI, smaller players must innovate or risk obsolescence.
2. **Healthcare**
   - **Example:**Google DeepMind's AlphaFold uses Generative AI to predict protein structures, accelerating drug discovery.
   - **Urgency:**Healthcare providers integrating AI today can lead tomorrow's breakthroughs.
3. **Finance**
   - **Example:**JPMorgan Chase leverages AI to draft investment reports, reducing time-to-market and improving accuracy.
   - **Urgency:**In a competitive market, adopting AI-driven insights can mean the difference between retaining and losing clients.

Challenges and Opportunities

While the potential of Generative AI is immense, challenges such as data readiness, ethical concerns, and workforce preparedness remain. Addressing these barriers requires:

- **Robust Data Infrastructure**: Generative AI thrives on high-quality, diverse datasets. Organizations must invest in data cleaning, labeling, and governance.
- **Ethical AI Practices**: As Generative AI becomes more autonomous, ensuring transparency and bias mitigation is critical.
- **Skilled Talent**: Upskilling teams to work alongside AI is non-negotiable. This includes both technical training and leadership development.

Is your organization prepared to overcome the barriers to Generative AI adoption, or are these challenges delaying your progress?

Getting Started with Generative AI

To stay ahead, businesses must move from planning to action. Here's how to get started:

1. **Identify High-Impact Use Cases**: Start with areas where AI can deliver quick wins—like automating customer service or personalizing marketing campaigns.
2. **Build Cross-Functional Teams**: Collaboration between data scientists, business leaders, and domain experts ensures AI initiatives align with organizational goals.
3. **Invest in Scalable Infrastructure**: Adopt cloud-based platforms like AWS or Azure to scale AI solutions seamlessly.

Generative AI Can't Wait

Generative AI is more than a technology trend—it's a catalyst for transformation. Organizations that embrace this paradigm now will define the industries of tomorrow. Waiting is no longer an option; the time to act is now.

Let's explore how organizations can prepare themselves to harness the full potential of Generative AI beginning with **Chapter 2: Building the AI-Ready Organization — Culture, Skills, and Mindset**

2

Preparing for AI Adoption – Building a Future-Ready Organization

"Culture eats strategy for breakfast."

Peter Drucker

As enterprises race to adopt Generative AI, it's becoming increasingly clear that success isn't just about algorithms, datasets, or cloud infrastructure—it's about people. The most cutting-edge technology will fail if the organizational culture isn't primed for change if leaders aren't aligned on strategy, and if teams lack the skills to operationalize AI effectively.

This chapter focuses on the human side of AI adoption, offering actionable insights for leaders to build resilient, AI-ready organizations. From fostering a culture that embraces innovation to equipping teams with essential AI skills, this chapter serves as a guide to creating an environment where AI initiatives don't just survive—**they thrive**.

Fostering an AI-First Culture

In the rapidly evolving landscape of Artificial Intelligence (AI), technology alone isn't enough to guarantee success. The most advanced models, powerful computing infrastructure, and well-structured data pipelines will fall short if the organization's culture isn't primed for AI adoption. This chapter explores the core principles of fostering an **AI-first culture**—one that empowers teams, promotes experimentation, and aligns every level of the organization with AI-driven goals. For leaders, this means embedding AI thinking into the DNA of their organizations.

What is an AI-First Culture?

An AI-first culture embodies the mindset that AI isn't just a tool—it's the foundation for how decisions are made, operations are optimized, and customer experiences are crafted. It's not about sprinkling AI on top of existing workflows; it's about weaving AI into the fabric of the organization, transforming how every department—from sales and marketing to HR and product development—approaches its work.

In an AI-first organization, the potential of AI to drive efficiency, spark innovation, and unlock growth is recognized at every level.

Key Attributes of an AI-First Culture

1. **Data-Driven Decision Making**
    - Strategies are no longer based on intuition alone. AI-powered analytics provide actionable insights to guide business decisions at every level.
2. **Experimentation and Adaptability**
    - Teams are encouraged to pilot AI initiatives, embracing both successes and failures as opportunities for growth. Iteration becomes the norm.

3. **Cross-Functional Integration**
    - AI is not siloed within data science teams. From HR leveraging AI for recruitment to marketing using AI for hyper-personalization, every department plays a role in adoption.
4. **Continuous Learning**
    - Employees are empowered to upskill and remain agile, keeping pace with AI advancements that continuously reshape the landscape.

A Real-World Transformation: Netflix as an AI-First Organization

Netflix's journey from a DVD rental service to a global streaming powerhouse illustrates the power of adopting an AI-first culture. When competition intensified, Netflix didn't just expand its content library—it turned to AI to deliver a hyper-personalized experience for every user.

- **Personalized Recommendations:**
    - Netflix's AI algorithms analyze user behaviors—what they watch, pause, or skip—to answer critical questions:
        - What genres excite this user?
        - What are similar viewers watching?
        - What content is likely to keep them engaged?

Impact: Over 80% of the content users watch is discovered through AI-driven recommendations, significantly reducing churn and boosting retention.

- **Data-Driven Content Creation:**
    - The success of House of Cards was no accident. Netflix's AI identified a high demand for political dramas and determined Kevin Spacey and David Fincher as strong audience draws. AI insights guided

the production, resulting in one of the platform's most successful shows.

Why Does an AI-First Culture Matter?

Netflix's success demonstrates that organizations that adopt an AI-first mindset can gain a significant competitive advantage. It's not just about improving operations; it's about reshaping how businesses think, act, and grow in an AI-driven world.

Is your organization viewing AI as a tool—or the foundation for its next wave of innovation?

Why Culture is Critical for AI Adoption

While AI tools and algorithms are essential, an organization's cultural readiness often determines whether AI projects succeed or fail. Here's why:

- **Breaking Silos:** AI thrives on cross-functional collaboration. Data from marketing, sales, and customer support must flow seamlessly across teams.
- **Empowering Teams:** AI adoption requires employees to trust the technology and feel confident using AI tools in their workflows.
- **Reducing Resistance to Change:** A strong AI culture reduces fear around job loss and focuses on the augmentation of human capabilities, not replacement.

Amazon's AI-First Mindset:

Amazon's adoption of AI goes beyond Alexa or its recommendation engine. The company integrates AI into logistics, supply chain forecasting, and warehouse automation. What sets Amazon apart isn't just the technology—it's the **AI-first mindset** across all levels, from top executives to warehouse workers. Employees are trained to rely on AI-driven insights for day-to-day operations, creating a cycle of continuous improvement.

Key Steps to Foster an AI-First Culture

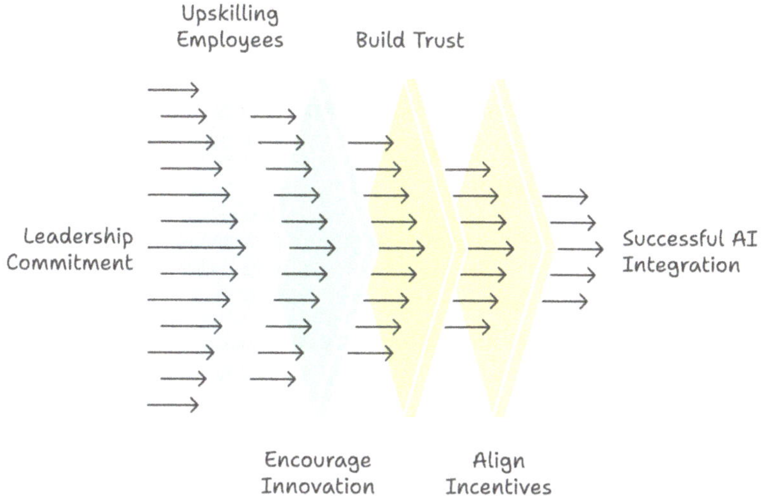

Step 1: Leadership Commitment and Vision

- AI adoption starts at the **top of the leadership chain**. Executives must not only champion AI initiatives but also set an example by using AI insights in their own decision-making.
- **Action Point:**Appoint a **Chief AI Officer (CAIO)** or create an AI governance council to oversee strategic alignment.

Example:
Microsoft's AI Transformation Journey:
Under Satya Nadella's leadership, Microsoft transitioned into an AI-first organization by embedding AI into all products and work-

flows, from Microsoft Office to Azure cloud services. Leaders were not just promoters—they actively showcased the impact of AI.

Step 2: Upskilling and AI Literacy

- Train employees at all levels—not just data scientists—to understand how AI tools function and how they can use them effectively.
- **Action Point:**Run **AI boot camps**, encourage **self-paced online courses**, and establish **peer-to-peer learning forums**.

Example:
Deloitte's AI Academy:

Deloitte launched its **AI Academy**, an initiative to train employees across roles on AI fundamentals, applications, and use cases. Employees learned to incorporate AI tools in auditing, analytics, and consulting.

Step 3: Encourage Experimentation and Innovation

- Create **AI sandboxes** where teams can run experiments with minimal red tape.
- Celebrate **failures as learning opportunities** rather than penalizing them.

Example:
Spotify's AI Hackathons:

Spotify conducts **regular AI hackathons** where teams are encouraged to prototype AI solutions. Many successful AI features, such as Discover Weekly and AI-generated playlist covers, started as hackathon projects.

Step 4: Build Trust Through Transparency

- Clearly explain **how AI tools make decisions** and communicate potential limitations.
- Involve teams in AI audits to ensure systems are fair and unbiased.

Example:
Salesforce's Ethical AI Framework:
Salesforce implemented an **Ethical AI framework** to ensure fairness and accountability in its AI-driven CRM tools. Transparency in model outcomes helped increase trust among both employees and customers.

Step 5: Align Incentives with AI Adoption

- Reward teams and individuals who **successfully integrate AI solutions** into their workflows.
- Provide recognition for **AI innovation and collaboration**.

Action Point: Include **AI-related KPIs** in performance evaluations.

Overcoming Resistance to AI Adoption

Even with leadership buy-in and cultural readiness, resistance is inevitable. Here's how to address it:

1. **Communicate the Benefits:** Show real examples of how AI improves efficiency and productivity.
2. **Address Job Insecurity Concerns:** Emphasize augmentation, not replacement, of human roles.
3. **Start with Small Wins:** Pilot smaller AI projects before scaling across the organization.

Example:
Rolls-Royce's AI Implementation:
When Rolls-Royce introduced AI for predictive maintenance in aviation engines, initial resistance arose among maintenance engineers. The leadership team addressed this by showing **how AI insights could reduce engine failures and improve flight safety**, turning skeptics into advocates.

Practical Blueprint for Building an AI-First Culture

Stage	Focus Area	Key Actions
Leadership Buy-In	Executive Alignment	Establish AI governance councils
Skill Development	AI Literacy Programs	Train teams across all roles
Infrastructure	AI Sandboxes	Build environments for experimentation
Trust & Transparency	Ethical AI Practices	Communicate model decision-making clearly
Reward Systems	Incentives & KPIs	Align team rewards with AI adoption goals

Measuring Cultural Readiness for AI Adoption

How do you know if your organization has successfully fostered an AI-first culture? Use the following metrics:

1. **AI Project Adoption Rate:** Percentage of teams actively using AI tools.
2. **Employee Sentiment Surveys:** Assess openness and confidence in AI tools.
3. **Innovation Index:** Measure the frequency of AI-powered experiments and solutions.

An AI-first culture isn't built overnight. It requires consistent **leadership commitment, structured learning initiatives, and a willingness to experiment and adapt**. Organizations that succeed in building this culture will not only thrive in the AI era but also become leaders shaping the future of business.

Skill-Building for AI Fluency Across Teams

> "AI won't replace people, but people who use AI will replace those who don't."
>
> Andrew Ng

In today's AI-driven landscape, **technology alone isn't enough**. For organizations to fully leverage the potential of **Generative AI**, employees at every level must develop **AI fluency**—a shared understanding of how AI works, what it can (and can't) do, and how to integrate it effectively into daily workflows. This chapter serves as a **practical guide for AI skill-building across diverse teams**, equipping tech managers and leaders with actionable insights to foster a culture of continuous learning and adaptability.

Why AI Fluency Matters Across Teams

Imagine a company where:

- Data scientists build sophisticated AI models, but business teams struggle to use the insights.
- Marketing teams attempt to personalize campaigns but lack understanding of AI tools.
- Leaders push for AI adoption without knowing the trade-offs or challenges involved.

This disconnect is one of the **most common reasons AI initiatives fail**. AI fluency bridges this gap, ensuring that **every team member understands their role in AI adoption and integration**.

Key Reasons Why AI Fluency is Critical:

1. **Alignment Across Functions:** Ensures consistency in AI adoption across departments.
2. **Better Decision-Making:** Empowers leaders with data-backed insights.
3. **Increased Adoption Rate:** Reduces resistance and accelerates AI deployment.
4. **Innovation Culture:** Encourages teams to experiment with AI use cases confidently.

Example:

At **Adobe**, AI fluency initiatives extend beyond the tech teams. Designers, marketers, and sales professionals are trained on Adobe Sensei, Adobe's AI platform, ensuring alignment across product teams and customer engagement channels.

Identifying AI Skill Gaps in Your Organization

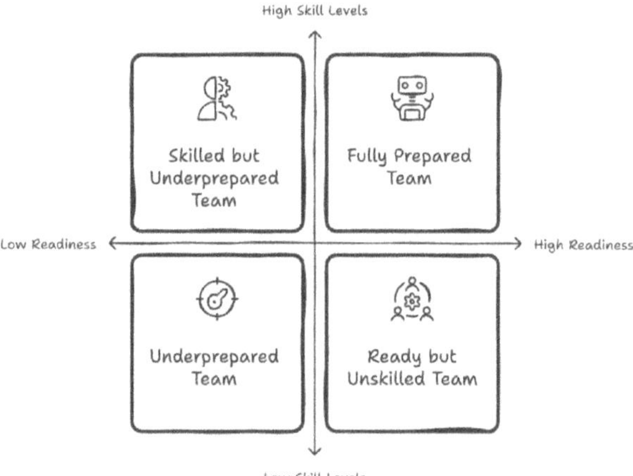

Before designing an AI fluency program, **leaders must first assess their organization's current skill levels and knowledge gaps**.

Conducting an AI Skills Audit:

- **Surveys and Interviews:** Understand team members' familiarity with AI concepts and tools.
- **Skill Mapping:** Identify specific AI-related competencies required for each role.
- **AI Readiness Score:** Use assessment frameworks to gauge team and organizational readiness.

Example Assessment Framework:

Role	AI Knowledge Level	Core Competencies Needed
Leadership	Basic	Strategic AI Vision, ROI Evaluation
Data Scientists	Advanced	Model Building, Fine-Tuning Models
Marketing Teams	Intermediate	Personalization, Campaign Optimization
Operations Teams	Basic	AI Workflow Integration, Automation Awareness

Building an AI Skill Development Framework

Step 1: Foundational AI Literacy for Everyone

- **What to Teach:**AI fundamentals, terminology, capabilities, and limitations.
- **Who Needs It:**Entire workforce—from frontline employees to C-level executives.
- **How to Deliver:**Workshops, e-learning platforms, AI crash courses.

Example:

At **Google**, non-technical employees are offered a course titled **"AI for Everyone"** to break down complex AI concepts into easily digestible modules.

Step 2: Specialized AI Training for Teams

Tailor AI training to suit the specific requirements of different departments:

1. **Leadership Teams:**
   - AI Strategy and Roadmap Development
   - Ethical AI Decision-Making
   - AI ROI Measurement
2. **Technical Teams (Data Scientists, Engineers):**
   - Advanced AI Model Development
   - Fine-Tuning Pre-trained Models
   - Monitoring and Scaling AI Systems
3. **Business Teams (Sales, Marketing, HR):**
   - Data-Driven Decision Making
   - Personalization Campaigns
   - AI-Powered Analytics Tools

Example:

Deloitte AI Academy provides role-specific AI training modules tailored to leadership, technical, and non-technical employees.

Step 3: Encourage Experimentation and Innovation

- Set up **AI Labs or Sandboxes** for teams to test AI tools without fear of failure.
- Introduce **hackathons and innovation challenges** to foster creative AI use cases.
- Recognize and reward successful AI initiatives.

Example:

Spotify's AI Hackathons have led to innovations like Discover Weekly and AI-generated playlist covers, directly enhancing user engagement.

Tools and Platforms for AI Skill-Building

Invest in **AI learning platforms and tools** to streamline skill-building efforts:

- **Coursera & edX:** Online AI certification courses from top universities.
- **DataCamp:** Hands-on AI and data science training.
- **Hugging Face Hub:** Collaborative platform for sharing pre-trained AI models.
- **Internal AI Knowledge Portals:** Centralized repositories of best practices, model documentation, and AI experiment results.

Creating a Culture of Continuous AI Learning

AI is a rapidly evolving field, and one-time training is insufficient. Organizations must promote **continuous learning and skill reinforcement**.

Best Practices for Continuous AI Learning:

1. **Regular Workshops and Webinars:** Host quarterly AI knowledge-sharing sessions.
2. **AI Mentorship Programs:** Pair experienced AI practitioners with new learners.
3. **AI Champions:** Identify and train AI ambassadors in each team.
4. **Stay Updated:** Encourage employees to follow AI research papers, blogs, and news.

Example:
At **IBM**, AI ambassadors within each team help disseminate AI knowledge, provide support, and ensure successful AI adoption.

Overcoming Common Challenges in AI Skill-Building

Challenge 1: Resistance to Change

- **Solution:**Clearly communicate the benefits of AI and provide reassurance about job security.

Challenge 2: Lack of Time for Training

- **Solution:**Offer flexible, on-demand learning options through online platforms.

Challenge 3: Limited Practical Applications in Training

- **Solution:**Include hands-on projects, real-world case studies, and practical use cases.

Example:
Airbnb's AI Training Programcombines theoretical learning with hands-on projects, allowing employees to immediately apply AI concepts in their roles.

Measuring the Success of AI Skill-Building Initiatives

AI skill-building must be **measurable and outcomes-focused**.
Key Metrics to Track:

1. **Training Completion Rate:**Percentage of employees who complete AI training programs.
2. **Knowledge Retention:**Pre- and post-training assessments.

3. **Real-World Application:**Number of AI-powered projects initiated post-training.
4. **Employee Sentiment:**Surveys to gauge confidence in AI skills

A dashboard as shown below may be useful to track progress and outcomes in AI learning and development.

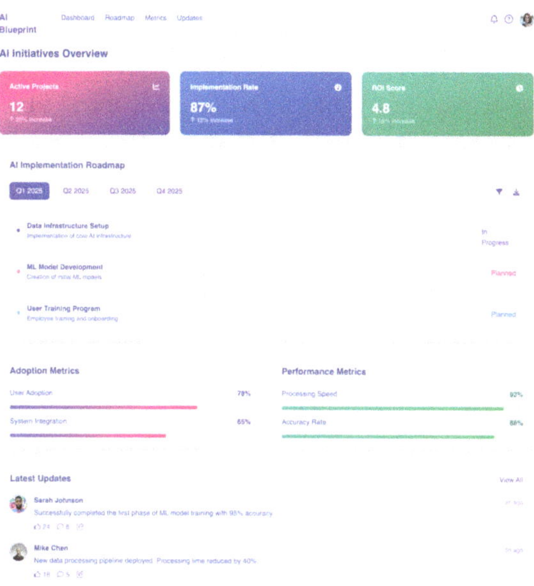

Fostering AI fluency isn't a **one-time effort—it's an ongoing journey**. Organizations that prioritize building AI skills across their teams will not only accelerate AI adoption but also create a **resilient, innovative workforce capable of navigating future challenges**.

Managing Resistance to Change

Implementing **Generative AI (Gen AI)** in an organization isn't just about upgrading systems or adopting new tools—it's about **transforming mindsets, workflows, and organizational culture**. Resistance to change is a natural human response, especially when employees perceive AI as a threat to their roles, autonomy, or established routines.

This chapter provides a **comprehensive guide to managing resistance to AI adoption** by addressing psychological, cultural, and operational barriers while offering **practical strategies for building trust, fostering collaboration, and ensuring successful implementation.**

Understanding the Roots of Resistance

Resistance to AI adoption can manifest at **individual, team, and organizational levels.** Leaders must first **understand the reasons behind resistance** before attempting to address it.

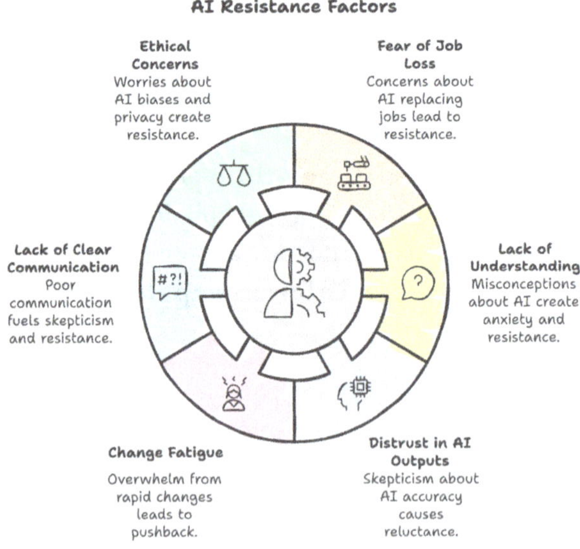

Common Causes of Resistance to AI:

1. **Fear of Job Loss:** Employees often fear being replaced by AI systems.
2. **Lack of Understanding:** Misconceptions about AI capabilities create anxiety.
3. **Distrust in AI Outputs:** Employees may not trust AI-generated insights or decisions.
4. **Change Fatigue:** Too many changes in a short span can overwhelm employees.
5. **Lack of Clear Communication:** Unclear objectives and poor communication fuel skepticism.
6. **Ethical Concerns:** Employees may worry about biases, privacy violations, or unintended consequences.

Example:

When **a leading European bank** introduced AI-based fraud detection tools, employees in traditional risk management teams resisted the adoption, fearing the new system would make their roles obsolete. Transparent communication and training on how AI complements human expertise helped ease the transition.

Building a Compelling AI Narrative

Create a Clear 'Why' for AI Adoption

Every AI initiative must have a compelling **"Why"**—a reason that resonates with all stakeholders.

- **Show Tangible Benefits:** Communicate how AI will improve efficiency, accuracy, and job satisfaction.
- **Align with Organizational Goals:** Tie AI adoption to company vision and long-term goals.
- **Emphasize Collaboration:** Position AI as an **enabler**, not a replacement.

Example:

At **Procter & Gamble**, leadership framed AI adoption as a tool to enhance creativity and reduce repetitive tasks, rather than as a cost-cutting mechanism. This positioning encouraged employees to embrace AI tools.

Develop an AI Adoption Roadmap

- Outline **short-term wins** and **long-term milestones**.
- Set **measurable KPIs** for AI adoption success.
- Communicate progress regularly to build confidence.

Leadership's Role in Overcoming Resistance

AI adoption isn't just a technology initiative—it's a **leadership challenge**. Leaders must set the tone and actively address resistance.

Key Leadership Strategies:

1. **Lead by Example:** Leaders should actively use AI tools themselves.
2. **Build Trust:** Be transparent about AI's role in the organization.
3. **Encourage Open Dialogue:** Create safe spaces for employees to voice concerns.
4. **Showcase Early Success Stories:** Highlight small wins to demonstrate AI's value.
5. **Invest in Training:** Equip teams with the knowledge and skills to work alongside AI.

Example:

When **Microsoft introduced AI copilots** for developers, leadership showcased real-world examples of productivity improvements, encouraging widespread adoption across teams.

Empowering Teams Through Training and Upskilling

Focus on Skill Development

Training is one of the most effective ways to reduce fear and resistance.

- **AI Literacy Programs:** Basic AI knowledge for all employees.
- **Role-Specific Training:** Tailored training for technical and non-technical teams.
- **Hands-On Workshops:** Allow teams to experiment with AI tools in a risk-free environment.

Example:

Deloitte's AI Academy provides role-based AI training programs, ensuring both technical and business teams feel confident using AI tools.

Foster AI Champions

Identify **early adopters** or **AI ambassadors** who can act as change agents within their teams.

- Champions help answer questions, provide guidance, and model AI adoption behaviors.
- They bridge the gap between leadership and employees.

Encouraging Experimentation and Safe Failures

Create Innovation Sandboxes

Allow teams to experiment with AI tools in **low-risk environments**.

- Build **AI Innovation Labs** where teams can test new ideas.
- Reward creativity and innovation, even when experiments fail.

Example:

At **Spotify**, innovation sandboxes led to features like **Discover Weekly**, which became a core part of their AI-driven product offering.

Encourage Cross-Functional Collaboration

AI projects often require collaboration between technical teams, product teams, and business teams. Foster **cross-functional teams** to break down silos.

Example:

Salesforce's Einstein AI platformintegrates data scientists, product managers, and sales teams in collaborative AI adoption workshops.

Continuous Communication and Feedback Loops

Communication is Key

- Create **AI Adoption Newsletters** to share updates and celebrate milestones.
- Host **town hall meetings** to address questions and concerns.
- Use **AI Dashboards** to visualize progress.

Establish Feedback Loops

Encourage employees to share their experiences and concerns about AI systems.

- Use **anonymous surveys** for honest feedback.
- Adjust training and processes based on feedback insights.

Metrics for Success: Measuring Adoption and Overcoming Resistance

Leaders must track **tangible metrics** to measure progress in overcoming resistance and driving AI adoption.

Key Metrics to Monitor:

1. **Adoption Rate:** Percentage of teams actively using AI tools.
2. **Training Participation:** Number of employees completing AI training programs.
3. **Employee Sentiment:** Surveys measuring confidence and acceptance.
4. **Innovation Output:** Number of successful AI-driven projects.

Shifting from Resistance to Advocacy

AI adoption is a **cultural shift, not just a technological one**. Organizations that address resistance proactively will overcome barriers and turn skeptical employees into **passionate advocates** for AI.

Building an AI Center of Excellence (CoE)

As organizations accelerate their adoption of **Generative AI (Gen AI)**, the complexity of managing AI initiatives across multiple departments, teams, and projects increases exponentially. An **AI Center of Excellence (CoE)** serves as the **nerve center for AI adoption**, providing strategic direction, governance, technical expertise, and standardized frameworks to ensure successful AI implementation at scale.

This chapter provides a **comprehensive blueprint for establishing an AI Center of Excellence (CoE)**, detailing its structure, roles, responsibilities, and operational guidelines. It also highlights **real-world examples** and **best practices** from leading enterprises that have successfully built their AI CoEs.

What is an AI Center of Excellence (CoE)?

An **AI CoE** is a **centralized organizational hub** responsible for:

- Defining AI strategy and vision.
- Building technical and operational standards for AI projects.
- Ensuring governance, compliance, and ethical AI practices.
- Upskilling employees and fostering AI literacy across teams.
- Scaling AI solutions across different departments.

Why Organizations Need an AI CoE

1. **Avoid Fragmentation:** Prevent siloed AI initiatives across teams.
2. **Accelerate Deployment:** Streamline processes for faster AI adoption.
3. **Ensure Consistency:** Maintain standardized tools, frameworks, and best practices.
4. **Optimize Resources:** Efficient allocation of talent and technology resources.
5. **Enhance Governance:** Establish ethical, responsible AI practices.

Example:

Microsoft's AI CoE drives AI innovation across products like Azure, Teams, and Microsoft 365 by providing cross-functional teams with shared resources, governance models, and standardized tools.

Designing the Structure of an AI CoE

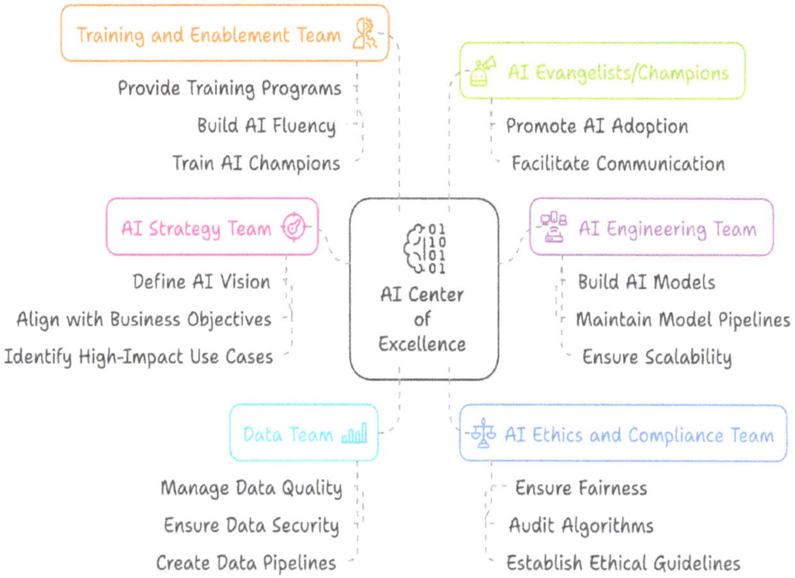

The success of an AI CoE depends on its **organizational design and operational model**. While the structure may vary based on the size and goals of the enterprise, certain roles and teams are essential.

Core Components of an AI CoE

1. **AI Strategy Team:**
   - Defines the organization's AI vision and goals.
   - Aligns AI initiatives with business objectives.
   - Identifies high-impact AI use cases.
2. **AI Engineering Team:**
   - Builds and deploys AI models.
   - Maintains model pipelines and APIs.

    - Ensures scalability and performance optimization.
3. **Data Team:**
    - Manages data availability, quality, and security.
    - Oversees data governance and compliance.
    - Creates data pipelines for AI model training.
4. **AI Ethics and Compliance Team:**
    - Ensures fairness, accountability, and transparency in AI systems.
    - Audits AI algorithms for unintended biases.
    - Establishes ethical guidelines for AI deployment.
5. **Training and Enablement Team:**
    - Provides AI training programs and workshops.
    - Builds AI fluency across all organizational levels.
    - Identifies and trains AI champions within departments.
6. **AI Evangelists/Champions:**
    - Promote AI adoption across business units.
    - Act as bridges between technical teams and non-technical stakeholders.

Key Functions of an AI CoE

Strategic Alignment

The CoE ensures that every AI initiative aligns with the **organization's strategic goals and vision**.

Best Practices:

- Regular alignment meetings with senior leadership.
- Define measurable KPIs for each AI project.
- Evaluate ROI from AI initiatives.

Governance and Risk Management

Establish **clear governance frameworks** to ensure responsible AI deployment.

Best Practices:

- Regular audits of AI models.
- Implement data privacy standards (e.g., GDPR, CCPA).
- Monitor and mitigate algorithmic biases.

Example:
At **HSBC**, the AI CoE monitors algorithmic fairness across all credit scoring models, ensuring compliance with global financial regulations.

Innovation and Experimentation
Create an **AI Innovation Sandbox** where teams can test and validate new AI ideas without operational risks.

Best Practices:

- Encourage cross-functional innovation sprints.
- Provide access to prototyping tools and frameworks.
- Celebrate successful AI experiments.

Training and Upskilling
Drive **AI literacy programs** for employees across technical and non-technical roles.

Best Practices:

- Organize workshops, hackathons, and AI bootcamps.
- Provide certification programs for AI fluency.
- Foster AI mentoring programs.

Cross-Functional Collaboration
Facilitate collaboration between **engineering, data science, business, and compliance teams**.

Example:

At **Spotify**, AI CoE acts as a bridge between product teams and AI engineers, ensuring music recommendations align with user engagement goals.

Implementing an AI CoE in Stages

Stage 1: Assessment and Planning

- Identify current AI capabilities and gaps.
- Define clear AI goals and objectives.
- Secure executive sponsorship and budget.

Stage 2: Build Core Teams

- Hire or upskill AI experts.
- Appoint AI champions in key departments.
- Create governance and compliance guidelines.

Stage 3: Develop Frameworks and Tools

- Standardize data pipelines and model deployment practices.
- Establish monitoring and feedback loops.
- Build reusable AI templates and APIs.

Stage 4: Pilot Projects

- Start with low-risk, high-impact pilot projects.
- Measure success against pre-defined KPIs.
- Document learnings for future scalability.

Stage 5: Scale and Optimize

- Roll out AI projects across the organization.
- Continuously improve processes and address roadblocks.

- Celebrate successes and share stories organization-wide.

Case Study: Building a Successful AI CoE at Walmart

Challenge:

Walmart struggled with fragmented AI initiatives across different business units, leading to duplication of efforts and inconsistent results.

Solution:

The company established a **centralized AI CoE**, consolidating AI talent, resources, and infrastructure into one hub.

Outcome:

- Reduced duplication of AI projects by 60%.
- Improved alignment of AI initiatives with business goals.
- Scaled AI models across supply chain, inventory management, and customer service.

Metrics for Measuring AI CoE Success

Key Performance Indicators (KPIs):

1. **AI Project ROI:**Tangible business impact from AI projects.
2. **Adoption Rate:**Percentage of departments leveraging AI tools.
3. **Innovation Index:**Number of new AI-driven innovations annually.
4. **Time-to-Deployment:**Average time taken to move AI models to production.
5. **Employee AI Literacy:**Percentage of workforce trained in AI fundamentals.

A dashboard as shown below would be useful to visualize the key metrics accurately.

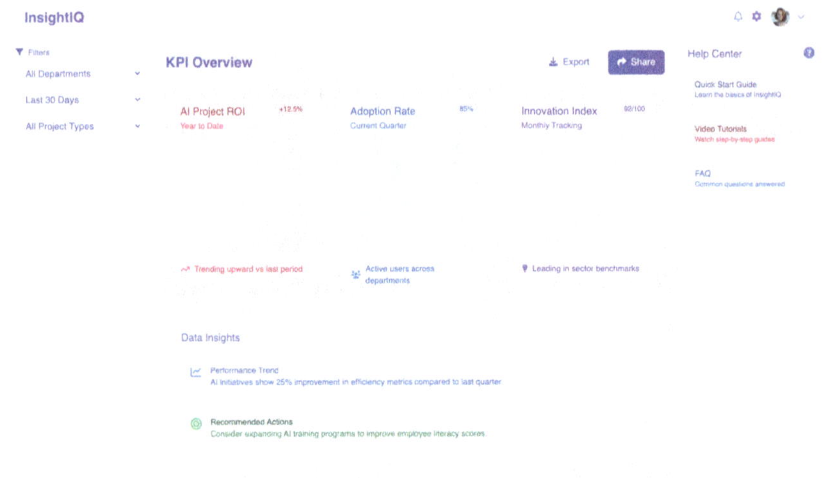

An **AI Center of Excellence isn't just about technology—it's about building organizational resilience, trust, and a culture of continuous improvement.**

By establishing a robust AI CoE, enterprises can:

- Ensure consistent and ethical AI adoption.
- Empower teams to innovate without fear of failure.
- Scale AI initiatives efficiently across the organization.

Measuring Cultural Readiness for AI Adoption – Assess, Align, and Accelerate

When it comes to **AI adoption**, technology is often seen as the star of the show. However, **culture**—the collective mindset, habits, and behaviors of an organization—determines whether AI initiatives will flourish or falter. Measuring **cultural readiness** is not merely about understanding employees' perceptions of AI; it's about assessing the organization's openness to change, leadership alignment, and the willingness to embrace experimentation and failure.

This chapter provides a **structured approach to evaluating and improving cultural readiness for AI adoption**, offering actionable insights, frameworks, and best practices to align culture with AI-driven objectives.

Why Cultural Readiness Matters in AI Adoption

The most advanced AI technologies are meaningless if the organizational culture resists them. A culture that fosters **collaboration, transparency, and a growth mindset** is essential for successful AI integration.

Key Reasons Cultural Readiness is Crucial:

1. **Trust in AI Systems:** Employees need confidence in AI outputs and decision-making.
2. **Adaptability to Change:** A culture comfortable with change embraces AI transformation faster.
3. **Collaboration Across Teams:** AI initiatives often involve cross-functional efforts between data science, engineering, and business units.
4. **Risk-Tolerance and Experimentation:** Successful AI adoption requires a safe space for experimentation and failure.

Example:

When **GE Aviation** introduced AI-driven predictive maintenance, success wasn't merely about algorithms—it was about training technicians to trust AI recommendations over instinct, fostering alignment between tech teams and field engineers.

Key Dimensions of Cultural Readiness

Cultural readiness can be assessed across several dimensions. Each dimension contributes to building an environment where AI adoption thrives.

1. **Leadership Alignment**
    - Are leaders committed to AI adoption?
    - Do leaders actively champion AI projects?
    - Is AI included in strategic discussions and decision-making?

Best Practice:

Ensure top executives set a clear AI vision and communicate the 'why' behind AI initiatives across the organization.

2. **Workforce Sentiment and Engagement**
    - Are employees excited or anxious about AI?
    - Do teams see AI as an enabler or a threat?
    - How willing are employees to upskill for AI?

Best Practice:

Conduct regular surveys and feedback sessions to gauge sentiment and address concerns transparently.

3. **Experimentation Culture**
    - Does the organization encourage experimentation and iteration?
    - Are teams empowered to fail fast and learn quickly?
    - Is there a system for capturing and sharing lessons learned from AI projects?

Best Practice:

Foster hackathons and pilot projects to create a safe space for experimentation.

4. **Ethical and Responsible AI Values**
   - Are teams aware of ethical considerations in AI deployment?
   - Are ethical guardrails clearly communicated?
   - Do teams understand AI's potential biases and how to mitigate them?

Best Practice:
Incorporate regular training on **AI ethics** and ensure policies are communicated organization-wide.

Tools and Frameworks for Measuring Cultural Readiness

Measuring cultural readiness requires a **structured framework** backed by qualitative and quantitative assessments.

a. **AI Cultural Readiness Scorecard**

An AI readiness scorecard helps evaluate cultural maturity across key dimensions.

Dimension	Assessment Criteria	Score (1-5)
Leadership Alignment	Active involvement, strategic clarity	4
Workforce Sentiment	Enthusiasm, openness, fear of job loss	3
Experimentation Culture	Tolerance for risk, pilot programs	4
Ethical AI Awareness	Training, adherence to guidelines	3

Example:
Salesforce uses a readiness framework called **AI Maturity Model**, which evaluates leadership, employee readiness, and technology infrastructure before launching AI projects.

b. **Surveys and Focus Groups**
   - **Anonymous Surveys:** Measure employee confidence and openness to AI adoption.
   - **Focus Groups:** Facilitate candid discussions about concerns, barriers, and expectations.

c. **Readiness Workshops**

Interactive workshops can be held to simulate AI-driven scenarios, encouraging hands-on exposure and addressing misconceptions.

Addressing Cultural Barriers to AI Adoption

Every organization will encounter cultural resistance to AI adoption. The key lies in identifying these barriers early and addressing them systematically.

a. **Common Cultural Barriers**
   1. **Fear of Job Loss:**Employees worry about AI replacing their roles.
   2. **Lack of Trust:**Skepticism about AI accuracy and fairness.
   3. **Resistance to Change:**Legacy mindsets resistant to new workflows.
   4. **Knowledge Gaps:**Lack of AI fluency across teams.

b. **Practical Solutions to Overcome Barriers**
   1. **Transparent Communication:**Clearly articulate AI's purpose and benefits.
   2. **Reskilling Programs:**Offer AI training and certification.
   3. **Celebrate Success Stories:**Highlight early wins and share AI success narratives.
   4. **Empower Champions:**Identify AI advocates in each department.

Example:

When **L'Oréal** adopted AI for product recommendations, they launched an internal campaign called **"Humans & AI Together"** to reduce fear and emphasize collaboration.

Building an AI-Accepting Culture: Practical Steps

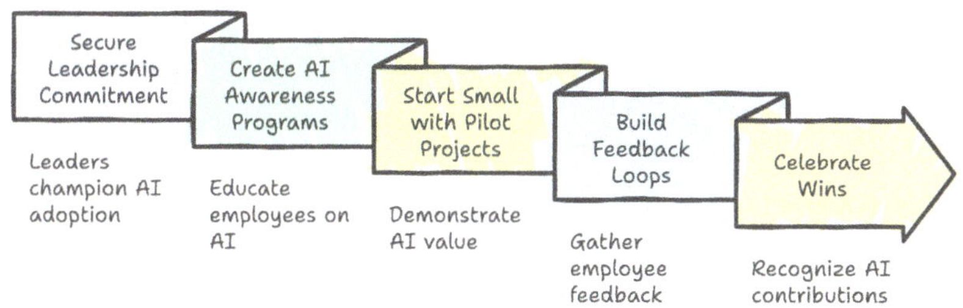

Step 1: Secure Leadership Commitment

Ensure top-level executives act as visible champions for AI adoption.

Step 2: Create AI Awareness Programs

Launch AI literacy initiatives across all organizational levels.

Step 3: Start Small with Pilot Projects

Select low-risk, high-impact AI projects to demonstrate tangible value.

Step 4: Build Feedback Loops

Regularly measure sentiment, collect feedback, and act on concerns.

Step 5: Celebrate Wins

Recognize teams and individuals who contribute to successful AI adoption projects.

Case Study: Adobe's AI Cultural Transformation

Challenge:

Adobe struggled with fragmented adoption of AI across departments, with resistance from legacy teams.

Solution:

- Conducted company-wide AI training programs.
- Appointed AI champions in each team.
- Established an **AI Ethics Committee** to address concerns.

Outcome:

- 70% of employees completed AI literacy training.
- Adoption of AI tools increased by 45%.
- Improved trust in AI-driven decision-making.

Key Metrics for Cultural Readiness

KPI Dashboard for Cultural Readiness:

1. **AI Literacy Rate:** Percentage of employees trained in AI basics.
2. **Employee Sentiment Score:** Survey results on AI perception.
3. **Adoption Rate:** Number of teams actively using AI tools.
4. **Experimentation Index:** Number of AI pilot projects launched annually.
5. **Ethical Compliance Score:** Compliance with AI ethics guidelines.

Cultural readiness isn't a one-time checkbox—it's an ongoing commitment to creating an **AI-friendly ecosystem** where teams feel empowered, informed, and confident about the AI journey.

When cultural readiness aligns with technology and strategy:

- Resistance fades.
- Adoption accelerates.
- AI becomes part of the organizational DNA.

The Human Advantage in AI Adoption

AI transformation isn't just about systems and software—it's about people. Leaders must invest in cultivating an AI-first culture, bridging the skill gap, and managing change effectively. Organizations that prioritize their workforce in their AI strategy will not only adapt but lead the AI revolution.

Let's move forward with clarity, confidence, and commitment to creating AI-powered organizations that are not just technologically advanced but also human-centric.

1. **ainability** to make AI predictions transparent.

Outcome:

- Regulatory fines were avoided.
- Patient trust increased with transparent AI predictions.
- The AI system became compliant with GDPR and HIPAA standards.

Tools and Technologies for AI Compliance

Tool	Purpose
IBM AI Fairness 360	Bias detection and mitigation
Google What-If Tool	Test AI systems for fairness and compliance
LIME & SHAP	Explainable AI tools for transparency
ISO/IEC 23894	Global compliance standard framework

Common Pitfalls in AI Compliance and How to Avoid Them

Pitfall	Solution
Overlooking AI compliance until deployment	Embed compliance at the design stage
Lack of skilled compliance professionals	Provide regular training sessions
Viewing compliance as a cost center	Highlight long-term ROI of responsible AI

Action Plan for AI Leaders

1. **Assess Current Compliance Status:** Run a compliance audit for existing AI systems.
2. **Build a Governance Committee:** Assign roles and responsibilities.
3. **Invest in Compliance Tools:** Use frameworks and software tools for automation.
4. **Document Everything:** Maintain comprehensive records of AI workflows.
5. **Regular Reviews:** Conduct periodic compliance reviews and audits.

Key Takeaway

- Compliance is a **business enabler**, not just a regulatory requirement.
- Proactive compliance ensures **trust, transparency, and resilience**.
- Use **robust tools and frameworks** for effective AI compliance management.
- Build an **organizational culture** that prioritizes ethical AI practices.

Transparency and Explainability in AI

The Importance of Transparency and Explainability in AI

As Artificial Intelligence continues to become a cornerstone of decision-making across industries, two fundamental principles have emerged as non-negotiable: **Transparency and Explainability**. While AI systems can process massive datasets, detect patterns, and make predictions at scale, their **"black box" nature** often leaves stakeholders—business leaders, regulators, and end-users—in the dark about how these decisions are made.

Transparency and explainability are no longer optional features; they are essential for:

- **Building trust** with stakeholders.
- **Ensuring fairness and accountability** in AI outcomes.
- **Meeting regulatory requirements** and ethical standards.
- **Facilitating adoption** across non-technical teams and decision-makers.

In this chapter, we'll unpack:

- **Why transparency and explainability are critical** in modern AI systems.

- **Key strategies and tools** for achieving explainable AI (XAI).
- **Case studies** showing successful implementation.
- **Practical steps** to integrate transparency into your AI workflows.

Let's decode the black box and build AI systems that are **understandable, interpretable, and trustworthy**.

Understanding Transparency and Explainability in AI

While these terms are often used interchangeably, they refer to **distinct but complementary principles**:

🔍 **Transparency:**

- Refers to the **openness of an AI system** in sharing its inner workings, data sources, and decision-making criteria.
- A **transparent AI model** allows stakeholders to understand how it operates and why it makes certain predictions.

Example: A credit approval AI should be able to reveal which factors—like income level, credit score, or spending behavior—were weighted most heavily in making its decision.

Explainability:

- Refers to the **ability of an AI system to provide clear and understandable reasons** behind its predictions or actions.
- Explainability translates complex AI outputs into **human-readable insights**.

Example: Instead of simply saying, "Loan rejected", an explainable AI system would provide reasons like:
"The loan was rejected because the applicant's credit utilization was 90%, exceeding the recommended threshold of 60%."

Why These Principles Matter:

- **Trust:** Stakeholders are more likely to trust AI systems they understand.
- **Compliance:** Regulations like the EU's AI Act and GDPR mandate transparency.
- **Accountability:** Clear explanations enable teams to fix errors and biases.

Tools and Techniques for Explainable AI (XAI)

Modern AI systems can achieve transparency and explainability through various **techniques and tools**.

1. **Feature Importance Techniques**
   - **SHAP (SHapley Additive exPlanations):** Assigns importance scores to features contributing to predictions.
   - **LIME (Local Interpretable Model-agnostic Explanations):** Builds interpretable models locally around specific predictions.

Use Case Example: In healthcare AI, SHAP can highlight which medical parameters—like blood pressure, cholesterol, or heart rate—most influenced a disease diagnosis.

2. **Model-Agnostic Approaches**
   - These techniques can explain **any type of AI model**, regardless of its complexity.
   - Examples include **Partial Dependence Plots**

(**PDPs**) and **ICE (Individual Conditional Expectation) plots**.

3. **Rule-Based Explanations**
   - For simpler models like **Decision Trees**, transparency is inherent because decisions are made via clear, step-by-step rules.

Example: A decision tree might say:
"If age > 30 and income > $50,000 → approve loan."

4. **Interactive Dashboards**
   - Tools like **IBM AI Explainability 360** and **Google What-If Tool** provide visual dashboards to interpret AI outputs.

Quick Checklist for XAI Adoption:

- Are you using SHAP or LIME for interpretability?
- Do your AI systems produce human-readable outputs?
- Are there dashboards available for stakeholders to interact with AI insights?

Case Study: Explainable AI in Financial Services

Scenario: A global financial institution uses AI to predict loan approvals.

Challenge:

- The AI model was highly accurate but lacked transparency.
- Loan officers couldn't explain to customers why their applications were rejected.

Solution:

- Integrated **SHAP** for feature importance scoring.
- Deployed an **Explainability Dashboard** for frontline staff.

Outcome:

- Loan officers could provide **clear justifications** for approval/rejection.
- Customer complaints reduced by **35%**.
- Regulatory audits became smoother and more efficient.

Challenges in Achieving Transparency and Explainability

1. **Complexity of AI Models**
    - Deep learning models with millions of parameters are inherently complex.
2. **Trade-Off Between Accuracy and Explainability**
    - Simpler models are more interpretable but may lack predictive power.
3. **Data Privacy Concerns**
    - Full transparency might reveal sensitive customer data.
4. **Lack of Awareness Among Stakeholders**
    - Non-technical teams may not understand the importance of explainability.

How to Overcome These Challenges:

- Use **model-agnostic tools** for interpretability.
- Educate stakeholders about XAI principles.
- Ensure **role-based access control** for sensitive information.

Are stakeholders in your organization trained to interpret AI insights?

Building Transparency into the AI Lifecycle

Transparency and explainability must be **baked into every stage** of the AI lifecycle:

1. **Data Collection:**
    - Ensure datasets are **well-documented and bias-free**.
2. **Model Design:**
    - Prioritize **interpretable algorithms** wherever possible.
3. **Model Training:**
    - Use **feature importance techniques** to understand model behavior.
4. **Deployment:**
    - Implement **explainability dashboards** for end-users.
5. **Monitoring and Feedback:**
    - Continuously monitor AI outputs for consistency and fairness.

Action Plan for Leaders

1. **Evaluate Current AI Systems:** Audit models for transparency gaps.
2. **Adopt XAI Tools:** Integrate tools like SHAP, LIME, and AI Explainability 360.
3. **Train Teams:** Provide explainability training for both technical and non-technical stakeholders.
4. **Embed Transparency in Governance:** Include explainability as a core compliance criterion.
5. **Document Everything:** Maintain transparency logs for auditing purposes.

Key Takeaways

- Transparency builds **trust and accountability** in AI systems.
- Explainable AI bridges the gap between **technical teams and stakeholders**.
- Use **industry-standard tools** like SHAP, LIME, and interactive dashboards.
- Embed transparency and explainability into **every stage of the AI lifecycle**.

Operationalizing AI Governance Frameworks

Turning Governance Principles into Actionable Practices

AI governance is no longer just a theoretical concept tucked away in strategy documents—it is an operational necessity. Organizations can no longer rely on high-level principles alone; they must **embed AI governance into everyday workflows, decision-making processes, and accountability structures**.

As enterprises increasingly rely on AI to drive innovation, optimize operations, and improve customer engagement, the risks associated with AI—**bias, transparency gaps, unintended**

consequences, and ethical pitfalls—also grow. Operationalizing AI governance frameworks ensures that AI systems are:

- **Ethically aligned** with organizational values.
- **Technically robust** and resilient against failures.
- **Accountable** with clear ownership and oversight.

In this chapter, we'll explore how to:

- Translate governance principles into **operational processes and workflows**.
- Build **clear accountability structures** across teams.
- Measure and monitor AI systems with **governance dashboards and KPIs**.
- Align governance frameworks with **regulatory and compliance mandates**.

Let's move from what we should do to how we actually do it.

Understanding AI Governance Operationalization

AI governance operationalization involves **transforming high-level governance policies into concrete, repeatable actions** across the AI lifecycle.

Key Elements of Operational AI Governance:

1. **Accountability Structures:** Define clear ownership and decision-making authority for AI systems.
2. **Process Integration:** Embed governance checkpoints into each phase of AI development—**data collection, model training, deployment, and monitoring**.
3. **Risk Assessment Frameworks:** Proactively identify and mitigate AI risks through **audits, reviews, and scenario testing**.

4. **Continuous Monitoring and Feedback Loops:** Implement systems for real-time AI performance and compliance monitoring.
5. **Training and Awareness Programs:** Equip teams with the knowledge to follow AI governance principles.

Example:

A healthcare provider using AI for medical diagnostics integrates governance by:

- Assigning a **Chief AI Ethics Officer**.
- Conducting **bias audits** every quarter.
- Ensuring **human-in-the-loop validation** for high-risk diagnoses.

Designing an Operational AI Governance Framework

An AI governance framework must be tailored to the organization's size, industry, and risk profile. Below is a **step-by-step guide** to design and operationalize an AI governance framework:

Step 1: Define Governance Policies and Standards

- Document **AI usage policies, data privacy rules, and model performance standards**.
- Align with **industry regulations (e.g., GDPR, HIPAA, AI Act)**.

Step 2: Identify AI Governance Roles

- **AI Governance Board:**Strategic oversight.
- **AI Risk Manager:**Risk assessment and mitigation.
- **Data Steward:**Data compliance and integrity.
- **AI Ethics Committee:**Ensure alignment with ethical principles.

Step 3: Integrate Governance into the AI Lifecycle

Phase	Governance Checkpoints
Data Collection	Data privacy compliance checks
Model Training	Bias testing and ethical reviews
Deployment	Algorithmic fairness validation
Monitoring	Real-time compliance dashboards

Step 4: Deploy AI Governance Tools

- **Audit Tools:**Validate fairness, bias, and transparency.
- **Monitoring Dashboards:**Track AI performance and compliance metrics.
- **Risk Assessment Frameworks:**Identify vulnerabilities across AI systems.

Case Study Example:

A **global retail company** operationalized AI governance by creating an **"AI Governance Playbook"** that defines key roles, workflows, and escalation paths for AI-related issues.

Measuring Governance Effectiveness

You can't manage what you can't measure. To ensure that AI governance is effective, organizations need **Key Performance Indicators (KPIs)** and **governance dashboards**.

Key Governance Metrics:

1. **Bias Detection Rate:** Frequency of detected and mitigated biases.
2. **Model Performance Drift:** Changes in model accuracy over time.
3. **Ethical Compliance Score:** Alignment with ethical standards.
4. **Audit Completion Rate:** Percentage of models audited annually.

Governance Dashboard Example:

- **Metric:** Data Privacy Compliance → 95%
- **Metric:** Models Audited Annually → 85%
- **Metric:** Ethical Breach Incidents → Zero

Does your organization actively track AI governance metrics, or is it a reactive process?

Aligning AI Governance with Regulatory Compliance

AI regulations are evolving globally. From **GDPR in Europe** to the **AI Act**, compliance isn't optional—it's mandatory.

Best Practices for Regulatory Compliance:

1. **Map AI Activities to Legal Requirements:** Align workflows with legal mandates.
2. **Conduct Regular Audits:** Ensure compliance through periodic assessments.
3. **Transparency Reports:** Publish annual AI transparency and compliance reports.
4. **Document Decision Paths:** Maintain records of AI-related decisions for auditability.

Example:

A **banking institution** maps each AI use case (e.g., fraud detection, credit scoring) to **regulatory requirements**. Regular audits ensure adherence to **AI Fairness Standards**.

Risk Management in AI Governance

AI governance must include **proactive risk management strategies** to address potential failures, biases, or unintended consequences.

Common AI Risks:

- **Bias and Discrimination:** AI systems may amplify societal biases.
- **Performance Drift:** Model accuracy degrades over time with changing data.
- **Regulatory Violations:** Non-compliance with data privacy laws.

Mitigation Strategies:

1. **Bias Audits:** Regularly audit training datasets and model outputs.
2. **Human Oversight:** Implement human-in-the-loop systems for critical decisions.
3. **Scenario Testing:** Test AI systems under extreme or edge-case conditions.

Practical Roadmap for Operationalizing AI Governance

Step 1: Start with a **Governance Maturity Assessment** to identify gaps.

Step 2: Create a **Governance Steering Committee** with cross-functional leaders.

Step 3: Develop **Standard Operating Procedures (SOPs)** for AI workflows.

Step 4: Deploy **AI Governance Tools** for auditing and monitoring.

Step 5: Foster a **Culture of Accountability** across teams.

Step 6: Continuously **Review and Update Policies** as regulations evolve.

Key Takeaways

- AI Governance operationalization bridges the gap between **policy and execution**.
- Clear **roles, responsibilities, and processes** are critical for success.
- Monitoring AI systems requires **governance dashboards and KPIs**.
- AI governance must align with **industry regulations and compliance standards**.
- Proactive risk management ensures **resilient AI systems**.

3

Practical Guide to AI Adoption for Enterprise Leaders

"The advance of technology is based on making it fit in so that you don't really even notice it, so it's part of everyday life."

Bill Gates

Artificial Intelligence (AI) is no longer a futuristic concept—it's a practical tool reshaping industries. But while many organizations are excited about AI's potential, far fewer know how to **move from strategy to real-world impact.**

This chapter bridges that gap. It offers **clear, actionable steps** to help leaders plan, prioritize, and scale AI initiatives effectively. Whether you're overseeing your first AI project or managing enterprise-wide adoption, this blueprint equips you with the tools to **cut through complexity and drive measurable results.**

Crafting an AI Strategy That Aligns with Business Goals

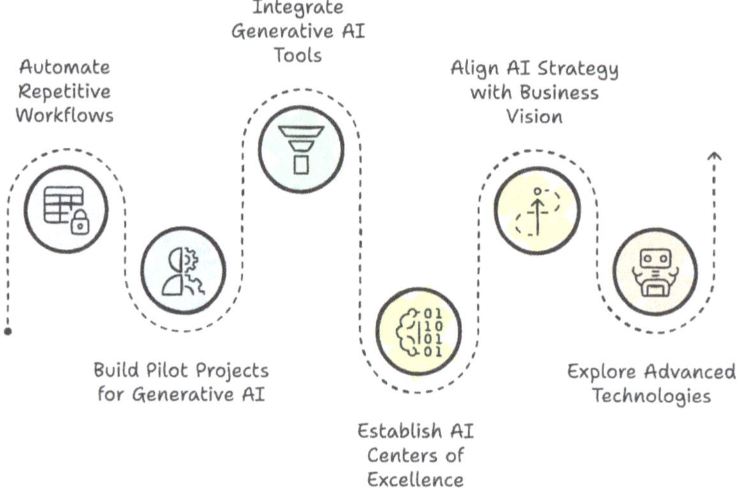

Why Start with Strategy?

AI isn't about chasing trends—it's about solving real business problems. Organizations that thrive with AI start by aligning their **AI strategy with their core business objectives.**

Three Pillars of a Strong AI Strategy:

1. **Clear Objectives:** Tie AI initiatives to specific business outcomes (e.g., reduce churn, optimize operations).
2. **Stakeholder Buy-In:** Get support from leadership, technical teams, and end-users.
3. **Scalability Focus:** Build systems that can scale across departments and geographies.

Quick Checklist for AI Strategy Development:

- Are your AI goals aligned with broader business priorities?
- Do you have measurable KPIs for each initiative?
- Is there clarity on short-term vs. long-term AI goals?

Identifying and Prioritizing AI Use Cases

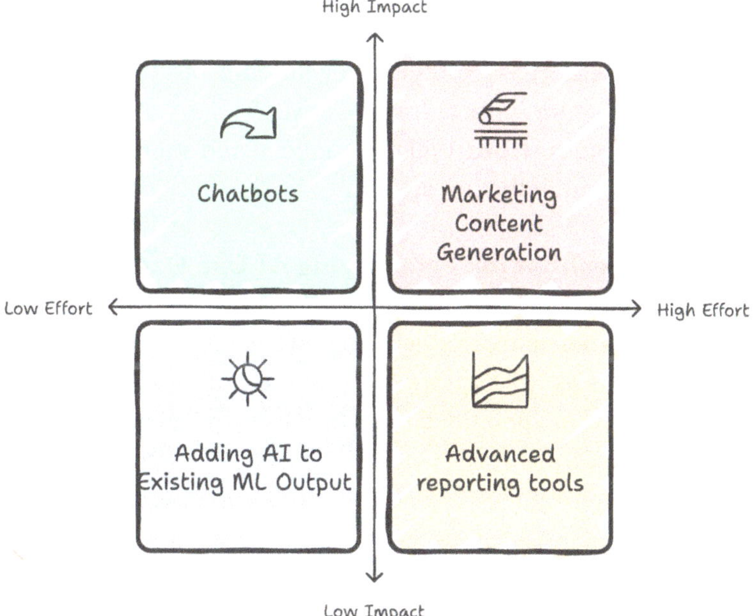

Not Every Problem Needs an AI Solution

One of the biggest mistakes organizations make is **deploying AI where it isn't needed.** Use the **Impact-Effort Matrix** to prioritize projects:

- **Quick Wins:** High Impact, Low Effort
- **Strategic Projects:** High Impact, High Effort
- **Avoid:**Low Impact, High Effort

Framework for Evaluating Use Cases:

1. **Business Impact:** What measurable outcome will this project achieve?
2. **Data Availability:** Is there sufficient clean, labeled data?
3. **Technical Feasibility:** Can your current infrastructure support this initiative?
4. **ROI Estimation:** Will the financial and strategic returns justify the investment?

Quick Checklist for Prioritizing AI Use Cases:

- Is the problem clearly defined and measurable?
- Are required datasets available and clean?
- Can ROI be quantified in terms of cost savings or revenue growth?

Example: A retail giant prioritized AI for **dynamic pricing** over an AI chatbot, as pricing optimization promised immediate ROI.

From Pilots to Full-Scale AI Deployment

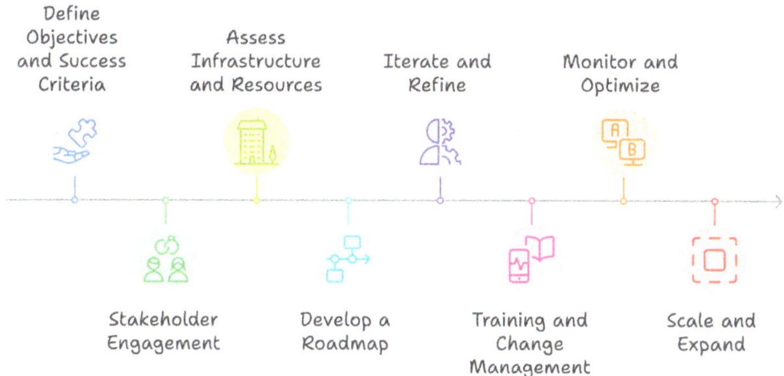

Bridging the Pilot-Production Gap

Many AI initiatives stall at the proof-of-concept (PoC) stage. Why? Because moving from **experimentation to deployment** requires robust processes and infrastructure.

Key Steps for Scaling AI Projects:

1. **Evaluate Pilot Results:** Were success metrics met?
2. **Standardize Workflows:** Build reusable templates for common AI tasks.
3. **Establish Governance:** Ensure accountability and ownership for every phase.
4. **Automate Deployment:** Use CI/CD pipelines for seamless updates.

Quick Checklist for Scaling AI Projects:

- Have pilot results been reviewed against KPIs?
- Are workflows standardized for repeatability?
- Is there a monitoring system for AI models in production?

Example: A telecom company scaled AI-driven **customer churn prediction models** from one region to their global customer base, leveraging standardized MLOps pipelines.

Implementing AI Governance in Enterprises

Operationalizing AI governance is a critical step for organizations adopting AI technologies at scale. AI governance ensures that AI systems are aligned with business objectives, ethical principles, and regulatory requirements while fostering trust among stakeholders. However, implementing governance in dynamic enterprise environments can be challenging, requiring clear frameworks, practical tools, and a cultural shift toward accountability.

Here's a roadmap to help tech managers operationalize AI governance effectively.

Why AI Governance Matters

AI adoption without proper governance is like piloting an aircraft without navigation. Unchecked AI can lead to biased outputs, security vulnerabilities, and compliance risks, jeopardizing organizational reputation and customer trust.

Before Governance

- Teams develop AI systems independently with little standardization.
- AI models produce results without clear explainability or audit trails.
- Regulatory compliance becomes reactive, leading to last-minute fixes and penalties.

After Governance

- Centralized oversight ensures consistency across AI projects.
- Explainable AI (XAI) tools help stakeholders understand decisions.
- Proactive compliance mitigates risks and streamlines operations.

Key Pillars of AI Governance

Building Trustworthy AI

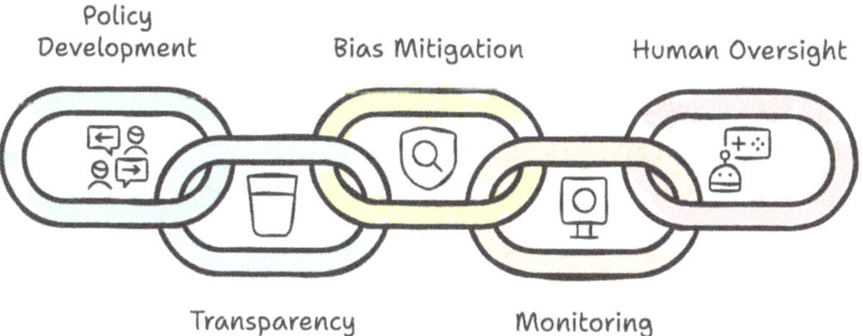

1. **Policy and Framework Development**
   - Establish enterprise-wide AI governance policies that define acceptable AI use, ethical principles, and accountability structures.
     - **Practical Example**: Develop AI policies specifying that customer data used for personalization must comply with GDPR and CCPA.
2. **Transparency and Explainability**
   - Use Explainable AI (XAI) techniques to make AI decisions understandable to both technical and non-technical stakeholders.
     - **Tool Spotlight**: Leverage tools like **SHAP** and **LIME** to provide feature-level explanations of model outputs.
3. **Bias Detection and Mitigation**
   - Ensure fairness in AI models by identifying and reducing biases in training data and algorithms.
     - **Emerging Tools**: Platforms like **IBM AI Fairness 360** and **Google's What-If Tool** offer automated bias detection.
4. **Monitoring and Auditing**
   - Implement AI monitoring frameworks to continuously evaluate model performance and ensure compliance.
     - **Real-World Use**: Amazon uses AI monitoring to ensure its recommendation algorithms remain unbiased and customer-focused.
5. **Human Oversight**
   - Retain humans-in-the-loop for critical decision-making processes, especially in high-stakes applications like healthcare or finance.
     - **Practical Tip**: Assign responsibility for model outputs to specific teams or roles, ensuring clear accountability.

Practical Steps to Operationalize AI Governance

1. **Centralize Governance Oversight**
   - Create an **AI Governance Council** consisting of cross-functional leaders from data science, IT, legal, and business units.
     - **Example**: Microsoft's AI, Ethics, and Effects in Engineering and Research (Aether) committee oversees ethical AI adoption.
2. **Adopt AI Governance Platforms**
   - Use platforms that integrate governance capabilities like monitoring, compliance reporting, and risk assessment.
     - **Tool Spotlight**: Explore solutions like **DataRobot's MLOps** and **SAS Model Manager** for streamlined governance.
3. **Standardize AI Development Workflows**
   - Use version control and CI/CD pipelines to ensure reproducibility and auditability of AI models.
     - **Example**: Git-based tools like **MLflow** help track experiment histories and enforce governance practices.
4. **Train Teams on Governance Best Practices**
   - Equip technical and non-technical staff with the knowledge to align their work with governance policies.
     - **Reflection Question**: Are all team members aware of the ethical guidelines for AI use in your organization?
5. **Regularly Review and Update Policies**
   - AI governance isn't static. Update policies to reflect emerging risks and regulatory changes.
     - **Emerging Trend**: AI-specific regulations, such as the **EU AI Act**, will shape governance policies in the near future.

After AI Governance: A Real-World Scenario

Before Governance

A retail organization deploys AI-powered dynamic pricing models. Initial successes are overshadowed by customer backlash as the models inadvertently raise prices disproportionately in low-income areas, leading to reputational damage.

After Governance

The same organization implements bias-detection tools to monitor dynamic pricing algorithms and ensures human oversight during implementation. As a result, the models adjust prices fairly across demographics, leading to increased customer trust and revenue growth.

Emerging Tools for AI Governance

- **Azure OpenAI Service**: Incorporates ethical guidelines for deploying large-scale models securely.
- **TruEra**: Monitors AI models for fairness, explainability, and compliance in production.
- **Pymetrics**: Ensures hiring algorithms remain unbiased using ethical AI principles.

Making Governance Actionable

AI governance isn't just a box to check—it's a foundational element of successful AI adoption. With the right frameworks, tools, and cultural mindset, enterprises can navigate the complexities of AI responsibly while unlocking its transformative potential.

Is your AI governance strategy keeping pace with the rapid evolution of generative AI capabilities?

Infrastructure and Technology for Scalable AI

The Role of Infrastructure in AI Success

Your AI models are only as strong as the infrastructure supporting them. Building scalable systems is crucial for AI to deliver results consistently.

Key Elements of AI Infrastructure:

1. **Data Architecture:** Use data lakes or warehouses for centralized storage.
2. **Cloud vs On-Premises:** Choose the right hosting model based on flexibility and security needs.
3. **MLOps Framework:** Automate training, deployment, and monitoring pipelines.

The MLOps Lifecycle:

- **Data Ingestion → Model Training → Deployment → Monitoring → Retraining**

Quick Checklist for AI Infrastructure Readiness:

- Is your infrastructure scalable and secure?
- Are there automated processes for retraining and monitoring models?
- Do teams have access to tools for collaboration and governance?

Example: An insurance company migrated its AI models to **AWS SageMaker**, enabling real-time retraining and monitoring.

Measuring Success: Defining and Tracking AI ROI

What Does Success Look Like?

If you can't measure it, you can't improve it. AI ROI is often evaluated across:

- **Cost Savings:** Reduction in manual labor or operational inefficiencies.
- **Revenue Growth:** Increased sales or market expansion.
- **Efficiency Gains:** Faster decision-making or improved workflows.

Build a Feedback Loop:

1. **Set KPIs Before Deployment:** Define success metrics upfront.
2. **Monitor in Real-Time:** Use dashboards for transparency.
3. **Iterate Regularly:** Optimize based on feedback.

Quick Checklist for Measuring AI ROI:

- Are KPIs clear and measurable?
- Is there a dashboard for performance visibility?
- Are lessons from failed initiatives documented and applied?

Example: A logistics company optimized routes using AI, reducing transportation costs by **15% annually.**

Cost Optimization in Generative AI Adoption

Adopting Generative AI presents unparalleled opportunities for innovation and growth, but it also brings significant cost considerations. For organizations, managing these costs while ensuring the effective deployment of AI is critical to sustaining long-term ROI. This section explores actionable strategies to balance innovation with financial prudence.

Strategies for Cost Optimization in Generative AI Adoption

1. **Optimize LLM Usage**
    - **Task-Specific Models**: Use smaller, task-focused models for narrowly defined use cases to minimize computational expenses.
    - **Token Efficiency**: Employ techniques like caching frequent outputs and prompt engineering to reduce token usage, which is especially critical for high-traffic AI applications.
2. **Hybrid AI Architectures**
    - **Balancing Tools**: Combine traditional machine learning (ML) and Generative AI to ensure cost-effective performance. For instance, ML can handle routine tasks like fraud detection, while Gen AI addresses complex use cases like personalized customer interactions.
    - **Example**: An insurance company can use ML for claims categorization and Gen AI for generating customer-friendly summaries.
3. **Adopt Open-Source Solutions**
    - Leverage open-source frameworks like Hugging Face's Transformers or OpenAI's API alternatives to avoid licensing costs while retaining the flexibility for customizations.
4. **Leverage No-Code AI Platforms**
    - Utilize no-code, open-source platforms such as **Make.ai** or **Lightning.ai** for rapid prototyping and experimentation. These platforms reduce the cost and time associated with building custom AI solutions, enabling fast validation of ideas without requiring large development teams.

- **Example**: A retail company can prototype a Generative AI-driven chatbot for customer support using Make.ai, testing its functionality and ROI before scaling to production.

5. **Optimize Hosting and Infrastructure**
   - **Cloud-Native Scalability**: Use cloud services that offer pay-as-you-go models, ensuring costs align with usage. Consider deploying AI models on edge devices or using compressed models for real-time applications to reduce hosting costs.
   - **Example**: Compressing models for edge deployment in IoT-based applications can significantly cut down data transfer and hosting expenses.
6. **Regular Cost-Benefit Analysis**
   - **Continuous Evaluation**: Regularly assess the operational efficiency and financial returns of AI initiatives. Use metrics such as cost savings from automated workflows or reductions in manual intervention.
   - **Example**: A healthcare provider using AI for predictive diagnostics can measure reduced patient wait times and operational costs versus ongoing infrastructure expenses.
7. **Train Teams for Cost-Conscious AI Implementation**
   - Invest in upskilling teams to optimize AI workflows with a cost-aware mindset. Enable cross-functional collaboration between tech and business units to balance performance and budget constraints.

Aligning Innovation with Affordability

Cost optimization in Generative AI adoption is not about cutting corners but about making smarter decisions. Leveraging no-code platforms for rapid prototyping, adopting open-source solutions, and combining ML with Gen AI are practical steps toward maintaining a balance between innovation and budget. By adopting these strategies, organizations can effectively scale Generative AI while ensuring a sustainable financial approach.

Are you leveraging cost-efficient tools like no-code platforms or open-source frameworks to reduce time-to-market for AI solutions?

Overcoming Challenges in AI Adoption

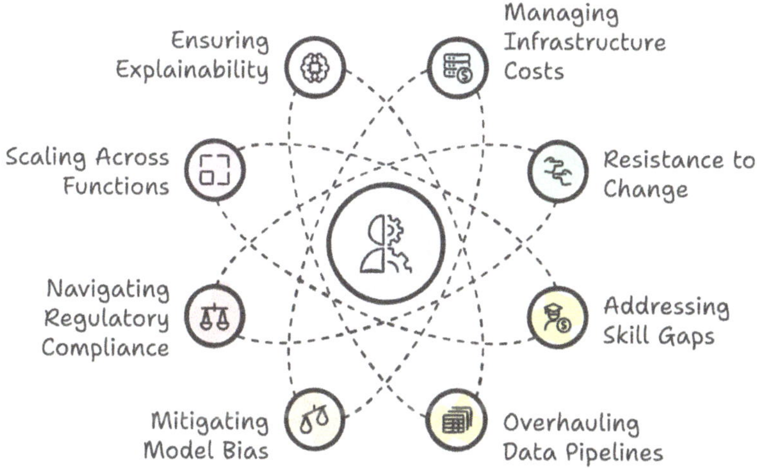

Adopting Generative AI comes with unique challenges that demand strategic action. From financial considerations to technical and cultural hurdles, here's a practical guide to overcoming them effectively.

1. Managing Infrastructure Costs

Challenge:

Training and deploying Generative AI models require significant financial investment in GPUs, hosting, and ongoing token-based expenses.

Solution:

- Use open-source frameworks to reduce licensing costs and fast prototyping .
- Optimize model usage with caching and efficient prompts to reduce token consumption.
- Hybrid AI Architectures
    - Combine traditional ML with Gen AI for specific tasks to balance cost and performance.
    - Example: Use ML for initial threat triage and Gen AI for in-depth analysis and response.

2. Resistance to Change

Challenge:

Teams may resist AI adoption due to fear of job displacement or skepticism about its value.

Solution:

- Educate teams on AI's role in augmenting, not replacing, human efforts.
- Highlight early wins with pilot projects to build trust.
- Develop "AI champions" to foster enthusiasm and act as internal advocates.

3. Addressing Skill Gaps

Challenge:

Organizations often lack sufficient expertise in AI, Generative AI, and data engineering.

Solution:

- Invest in upskilling programs for employees using platforms like **Coursera** or **edX.**
- Hire AI specialists or partner with universities for talent pipelines.
- Foster cross-functional collaboration to align technical and business objectives.

4. Overhauling Data Pipelines

Challenge:

Legacy data systems often fail to meet the requirements for real-time, high-quality data.

Solution:

- Upgrade to modern data platforms like Snowflake or Google BigQuery.
- Implement strict data governance for regulatory compliance and data quality.
- Automate data integration with tools like Apache Airflow.

5. Mitigating Model Bias

Challenge:

AI models may unintentionally reinforce biases in training data, leading to unfair or harmful outcomes.

Solution:

- Use bias detection tools like IBM's AI Fairness 360 to monitor and reduce bias.
- Regularly audit training datasets for inclusivity and representativeness.
- Involve diverse teams during model development to ensure balanced perspectives.

6. Navigating Regulatory Compliance

Challenge:

Generative AI systems must comply with evolving regulations like GDPR or CCPA.

Solution:

- Build compliance checkpoints into AI workflows.
- Leverage AI tools for automated audit trails and real-time compliance monitoring.
- Consult legal experts during deployment phases to preempt violations.

7. Scaling Across Functions

Challenge:

Adopting AI enterprise-wide can be complex due to differing departmental needs.

Solution:

- Create modular AI systems that can adapt to multiple use cases.
- Establish an AI Center of Excellence (CoE) to streamline scaling and knowledge sharing.
- Start with high-impact areas to demonstrate value before scaling.

8. Ensuring Explainability

Challenge:

Non-technical stakeholders may struggle to trust or understand AI-generated insights.

Solution:

- Use explainable AI (XAI) frameworks like SHAP or LIME to make predictions transparent.
- Provide narrative outputs alongside metrics for business leaders.
- Train teams to interpret and communicate AI findings effectively.

Turning Challenges into Opportunities

Each challenge presents an opportunity for growth and improvement. Leaders who address these hurdles with practical strategies will not only overcome barriers but also position their organizations for sustained success in the AI era.

- Have you aligned your AI strategy with the resources and readiness of your organization?
- Is there a plan to continuously upskill employees?

Action Plan: Next Steps for AI Adoption

1. **Define Goals:** Tie AI initiatives to specific, measurable outcomes.
2. **Prioritize Use Cases:** Focus on high-impact, low-effort projects first.
3. **Invest in Infrastructure:** Build scalable and secure data systems.
4. **Build MLOps Pipelines:** Automate model deployment and monitoring.
5. **Track Success:** Regularly measure and optimize AI initiatives.

AI adoption isn't just about tools and technology—it's about aligning strategy, people, and processes to create lasting value.

4

Essential Generative AI Terms Every Leader Must Know

"Knowing AI jargon isn't about impressing in meetings; it's about making informed decisions in a rapidly evolving tech landscape."

Fei-Fei Li

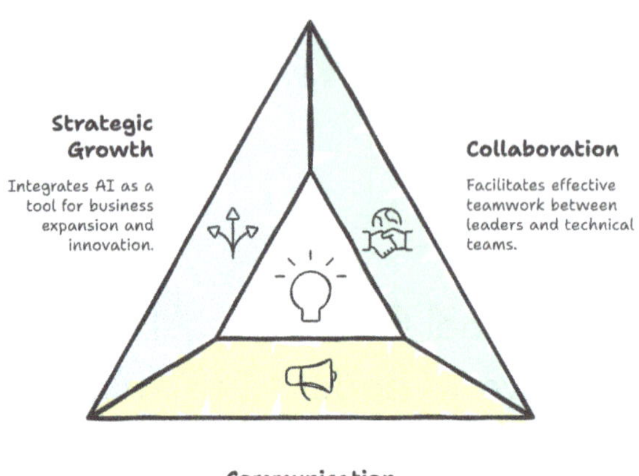

Understanding the foundational concepts of generative AI is no longer a luxury—it's a necessity for tech and business managers steering AI adoption in mid-to-large enterprises. This section distills the most impactful AI terms into digestible insights, equipping leaders to collaborate effectively with technical teams, communicate with stakeholders, and harness AI's transformative power. By demystifying these core ideas, businesses can move from experimenting with AI to embedding it as a strategic tool for growth.

By unpacking these terms, tech and business managers can better understand how generative AI systems work, paving the way for informed decision-making and strategic alignment. In the next section, we'll dive deeper into specific keywords and practical use cases, equipping you with actionable insights to drive AI success.

Large Language Model (LLM)

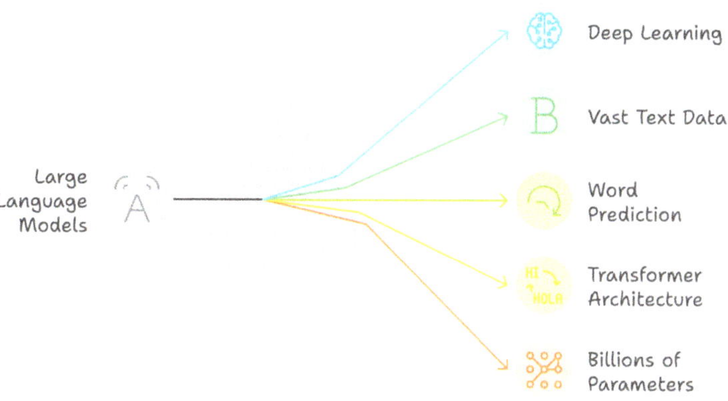

LLMs are expansive models trained on vast datasets of human language. They excel at text generation, answering questions, and performing language tasks, forming the backbone of technologies like chatbots and voice assistants.

Example: GPT-4, Bard, and Llama 2 are prominent examples of LLMs.

A retail customer support chatbot leverages LLMs to handle nuanced queries, providing accurate and timely responses, boosting satisfaction.

HR teams use LLMs to craft culturally nuanced job descriptions, streamlining hiring processes.

LLMs are the cornerstone of generative AI, driving breakthroughs in automation and personalized user interactions.

Transformer Model

Building Blocks of Transformer Success

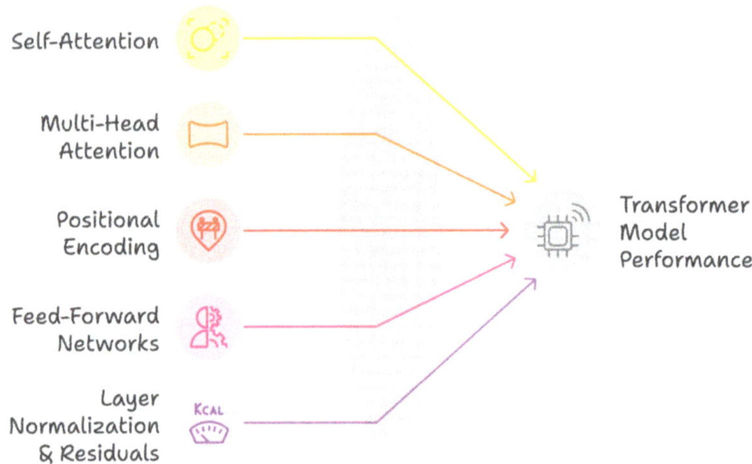

Transformers are the foundational architecture for LLMs, enabling them to process text, identify relevant information, and deliver contextually accurate responses. Their ability to focus on specific parts of input data (via "attention mechanisms") makes them versatile.

Example: The Transformer architecture is the foundation for models like BERT and GPT, enabling them to achieve state-of-the-art performance in various NLP tasks

A restaurant chain uses transformers to analyze social media reviews, flagging consistent feedback like “long wait times” for actionable insights.

Legal firms employ transformers to summarize lengthy contracts, highlighting critical clauses and saving hours of manual effort.

Transformers make sense of unstructured data, delivering insights faster and more effectively than traditional models.

RAG (Retrieval-Augmented Generation)

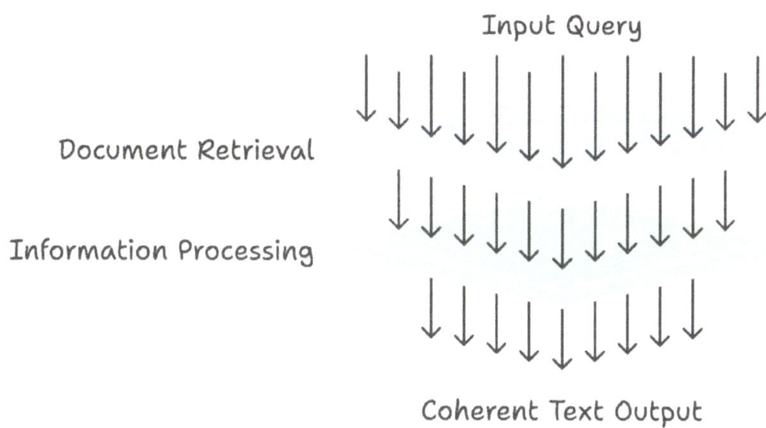

RAG enhances AI responses by integrating retrieved information from a knowledge base into generated text. This method ensures responses are accurate, relevant, and conversational.

Example: A chatbot using RAG can access and incorporate information from a company's knowledge base or a customer relationship management (CRM) system to provide more accurate and personalized response.

E-commerce chatbots use RAG to fetch and explain product specs directly from the catalog, ensuring precise answers.

RAG combines data retrieval with language generation, creating AI solutions that are both informed and engaging.

Intent Extraction

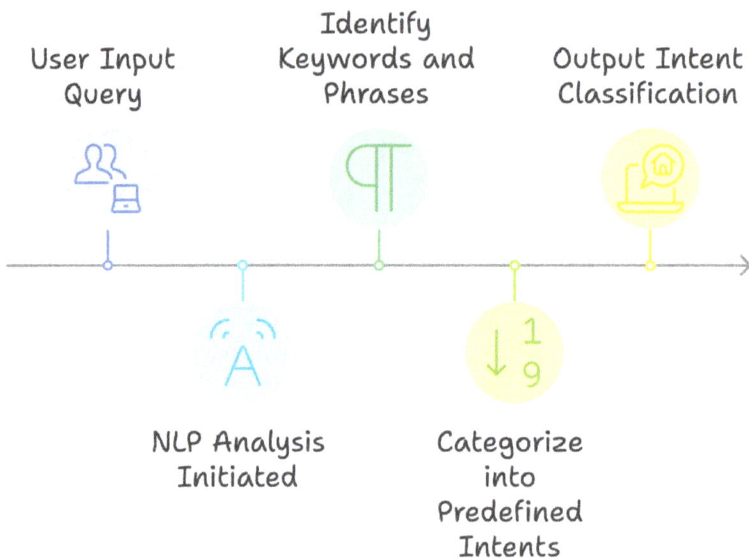

Intent extraction identifies the purpose behind a user's query, enabling AI to respond effectively. It's vital for chatbots and other systems requiring clarity and precision.

Example 1: An online store uses intent detection to differentiate between a customer's inquiry about product availability and a return request.

Example 2: Financial institutions extract intent to separate loan inquiries from account-related questions, routing each to the appropriate system.

By understanding intent, businesses can tailor responses to customer needs, improving efficiency and satisfaction.

Embedding

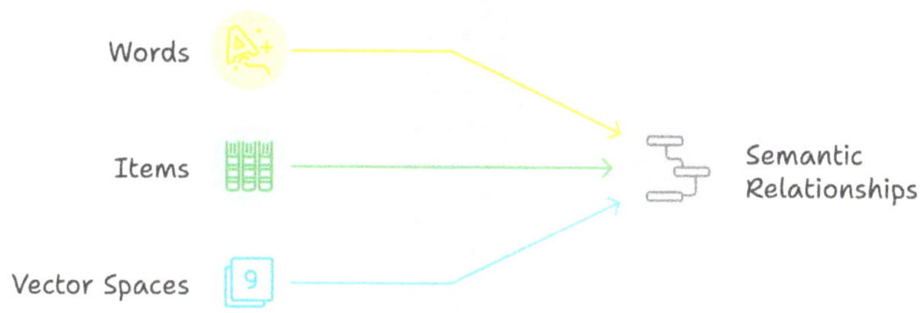

Embeddings are vector representations of data, capturing relationships between items or terms. They are essential for similarity searches and recommendation engines.

Example: Word embeddings like Word2Vec and GloVe allow computers to understand the relationships between words, such as "king" is to "man" as "queen" is to "woman."

Retailers analyze embeddings to recommend complementary products based on a customer's purchase history.

Embeddings unlock the power of personalization, connecting users with relevant content seamlessly.

Vector Store

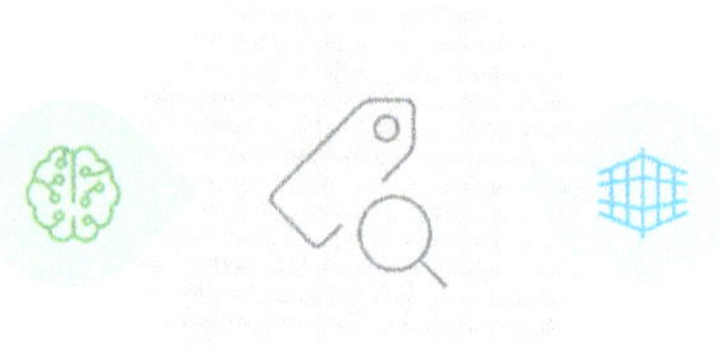

Vector stores store and retrieve embeddings for quick, scalable similarity searches, essential for real-time applications.

Example 1: Streaming services use vector stores to find similar movies or shows for personalized viewing recommendations.

Example 2: E-commerce platforms rely on vector stores to suggest alternative products based on a customer's browsing history.

Vector stores enable real-time personalization, creating better user experiences.

ChromaDB, Pinecone, AWS Qdrant etc., are some the prominent vector databases available.

Fine-Tuning

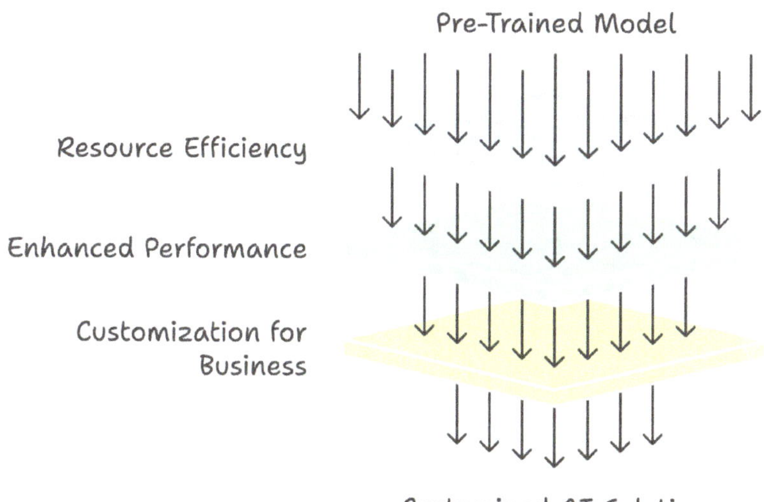

Fine-tuning adapts pre-trained models to specific tasks using targeted data, allowing businesses to leverage AI for unique challenges without starting from scratch.

Example: A pre-trained LLM like GPT-3 can be fine-tuned to generate marketing copy, write code, or answer questions specific to a particular industry

Financial firms refine AI to detect fraud patterns unique to their operations.

Fine-tuning ensures AI solutions are relevant, precise, and aligned with business objectives.

Attention Mechanism

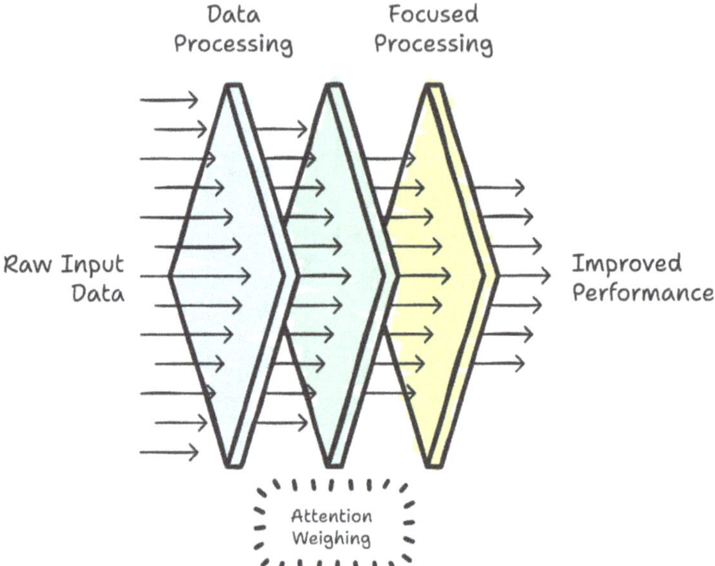

Attention mechanisms help models focus on the most relevant parts of input data, improving the accuracy of responses and insights.

Example 1: AI in customer service identifies and prioritizes key terms like "urgent" or "refund" in support tickets.

Example 2: Legal tech tools use attention mechanisms to highlight critical phrases in contracts, aiding faster analysis.

This capability ensures AI solutions deliver focused, high-quality outputs.

llmOps

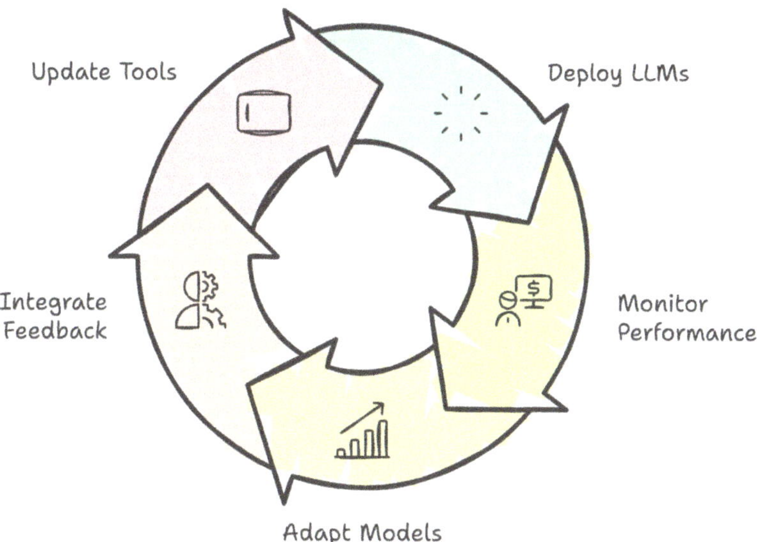

llmOps involves the management, monitoring, and optimization of LLMs in production environments, ensuring reliability and consistent performance.

Example 1: An online retailer uses llmOps to monitor chatbot accuracy and optimize response times during peak sales seasons.

Example 2: A banking app leverages llmOps to ensure its virtual assistant maintains efficiency and relevance.

Effective llmOps ensures the smooth functioning of AI models in live environments.

Context Window / Context Length

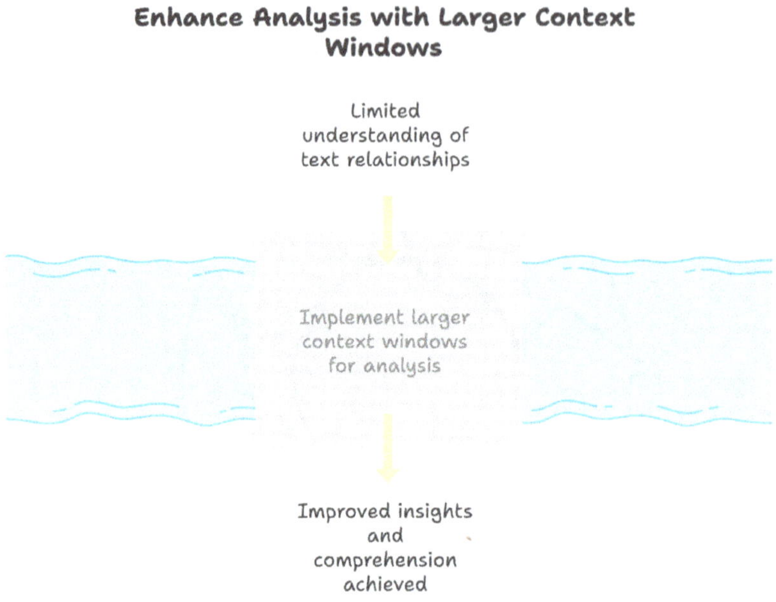

Enhance Analysis with Larger Context Windows

Limited understanding of text relationships

Implement larger context windows for analysis

Improved insights and comprehension achieved

The context window determines how much information an AI model can consider at a time. Larger windows allow for better handling of extended conversations or document analysis.

Example 1: Customer support AI leverages larger context windows to maintain coherence across multi-turn conversations.

Example 2: Legal AI uses extended context windows to analyze and summarize lengthy contracts without losing context.

A broader context window improves AI's ability to deliver nuanced, accurate responses in complex scenarios.

Tokenization

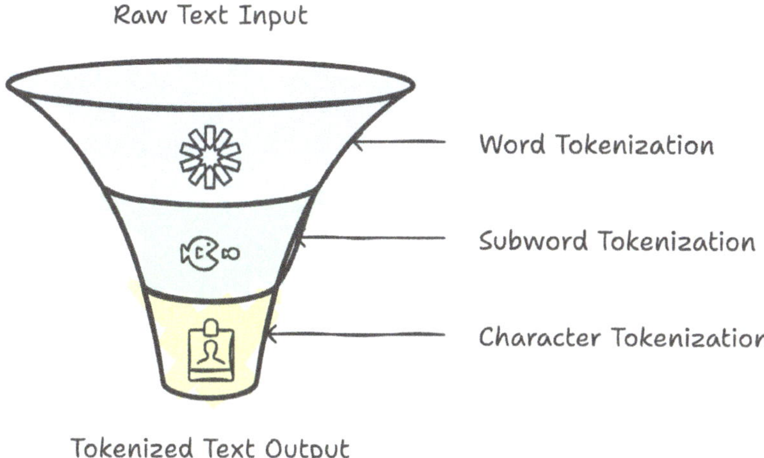

Tokenization is the process of breaking down text into smaller units, or "tokens," such as words, phrases, or even individual characters. This is foundational for any language-based AI task, enabling models to process and understand text more effectively.

Example 1: In customer support, tokenization helps classify phrases like "payment failed" or "login issue," ensuring the query is routed to the correct department.

Example 2: Social media platforms use tokenization to analyze trending hashtags and keywords, helping marketers identify real-time trends.

Tokenization is foundational for natural language processing (NLP) tasks. It allows AI to analyze and interpret text efficiently, ensuring context-aware and accurate outputs.

Reinforcement Learning from Human Feedback (RLHF)

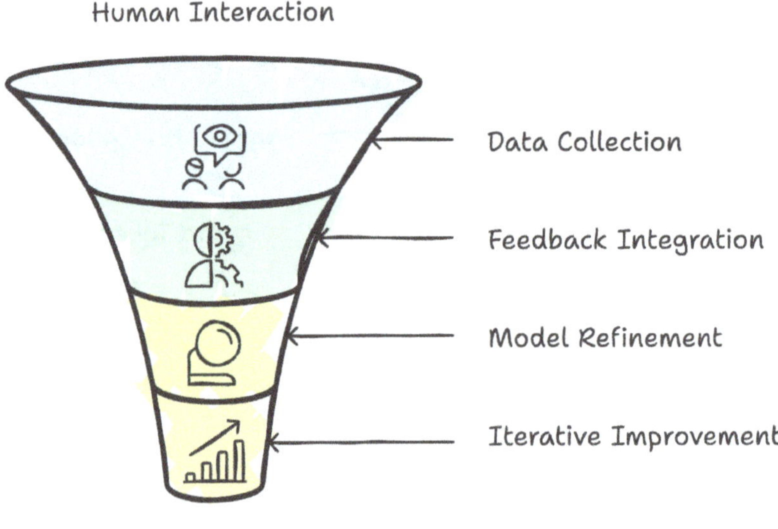

RLHF is a training method where human feedback refines an AI model's performance. By aligning model outputs with user expectations, RLHF ensures that AI systems are adaptive and precise.

Example 1: Customer service bots improve their responses based on real-time feedback, enhancing user satisfaction.

Example 2: In financial services, RLHF helps AI-generated advice align with client-specific investment preferences.

RLHF bridges the gap between raw AI outputs and nuanced human understanding, making AI more effective in dynamic, real-world applications.

Diffusion Models

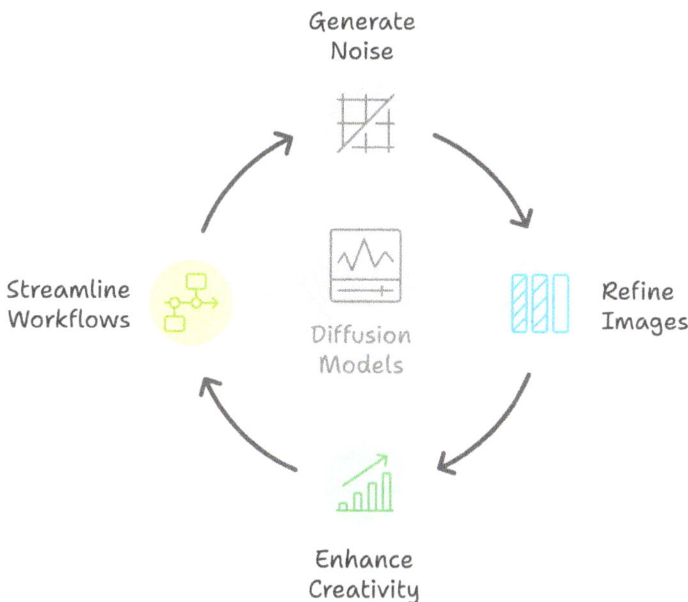

Diffusion models iteratively refine noise to generate stunning images. This technology is a game-changer in design, marketing, and creative industries.

Example 1: Marketing teams use diffusion models to generate unique visuals for ad campaigns, reducing reliance on stock images.

Example 2: Automotive companies employ diffusion models to create concept car renderings, accelerating the design process.

These models enable businesses to create unique, high-resolution visuals quickly, reducing reliance on costly design processes and sparking innovation.

Personalization

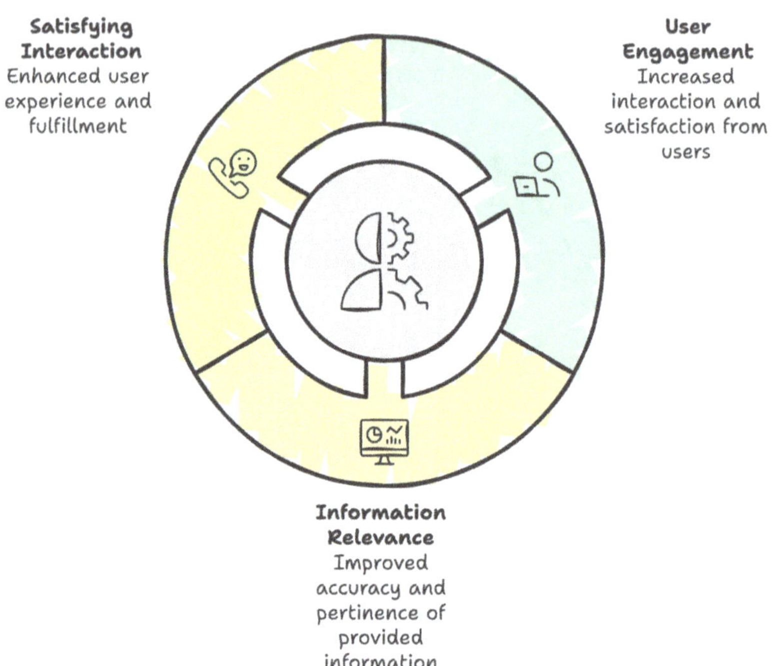

Personalization allows AI systems to adapt their outputs to user preferences, significantly enhancing engagement and relevance.

Example 1: Streaming platforms recommend shows based on a user's watch history, boosting viewer retention.

Example 2: E-commerce platforms suggest products aligned with a customer's past purchases, increasing conversion rates.

In a crowded digital marketplace, personalization increases customer loyalty and conversion rates by delivering tailored experiences.

Hallucination

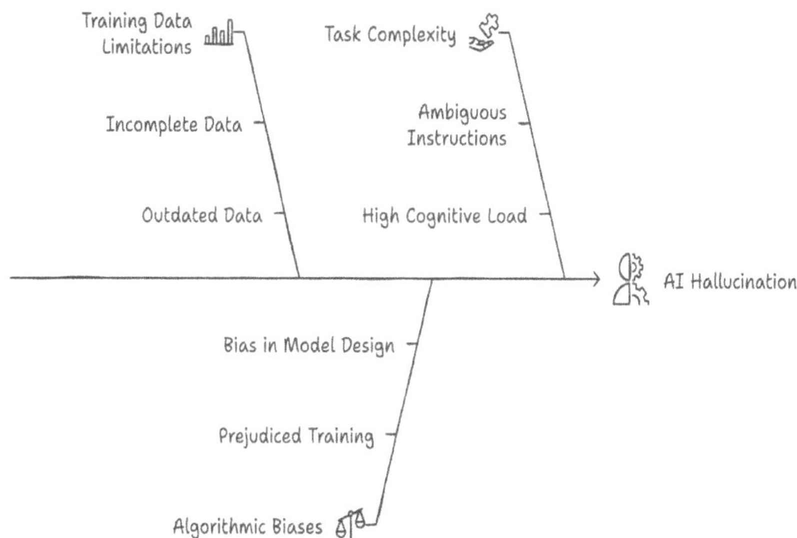

Hallucination occurs when AI generates incorrect or fabricated information. Addressing this is crucial for building trust, especially in critical industries like finance and healthcare.

Example: An LLM might "hallucinate" facts or invent information when generating

Financial chatbots might hallucinate outdated policy details, underlining the importance of validation mechanisms.

Preventing hallucinations ensures trust in AI, particularly in industries like finance and healthcare, where accuracy is paramount.

Human-in-the-Loop (HITL)

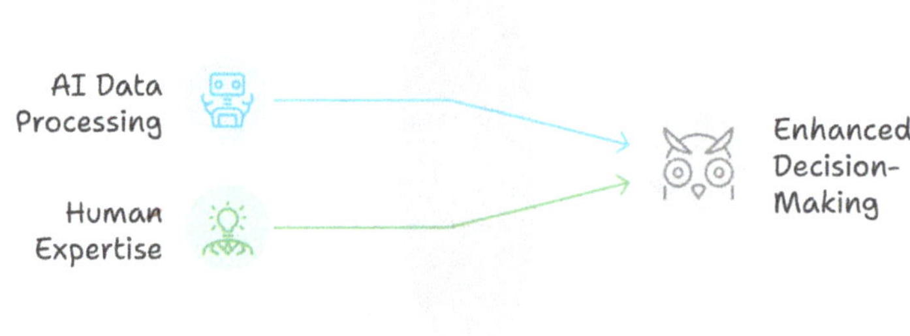

HITL systems integrate human judgment into AI workflows to verify outputs, especially in high-stakes applications. This ensures AI aligns with business objectives and regulatory requirements.

Example 1: Radiologists review AI-generated imaging results to confirm diagnoses, combining speed with accuracy.

Example 2: Financial advisors validate AI-driven investment recommendations before presenting them to clients.

HITL integrates human oversight into AI workflows, ensuring alignment with business goals and regulatory standards.

Guardrails

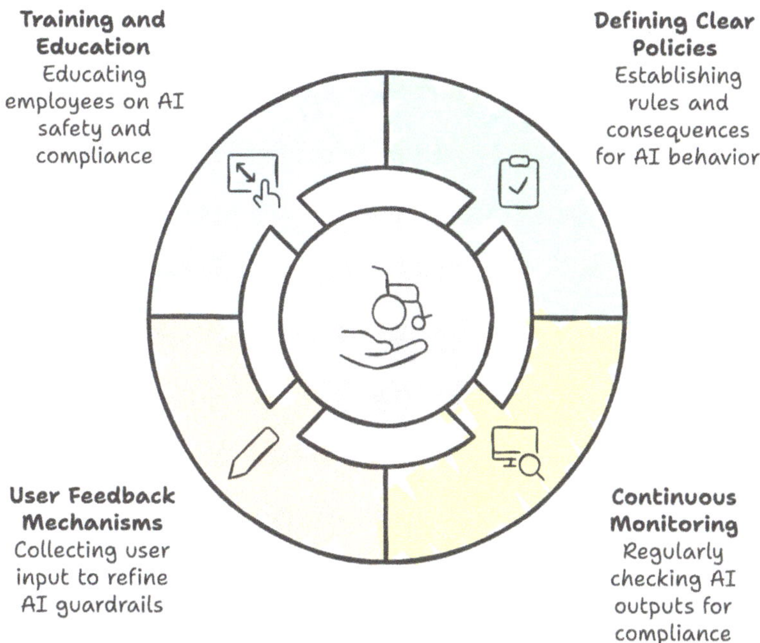

Guardrails define the boundaries of AI behavior, ensuring outputs are safe, compliant, and aligned with organizational goals. These are especially critical in customer-facing or regulated environments.

Example 1: Banking chatbots use guardrails to avoid discussing sensitive financial topics beyond their scope.

Example 2: Retail AI applies guardrails to ensure chatbots do not recommend products that are out of stock.

Guardrails prevent unintended consequences by limiting AI behavior, protecting both the brand and the end user.

Safety Constraints

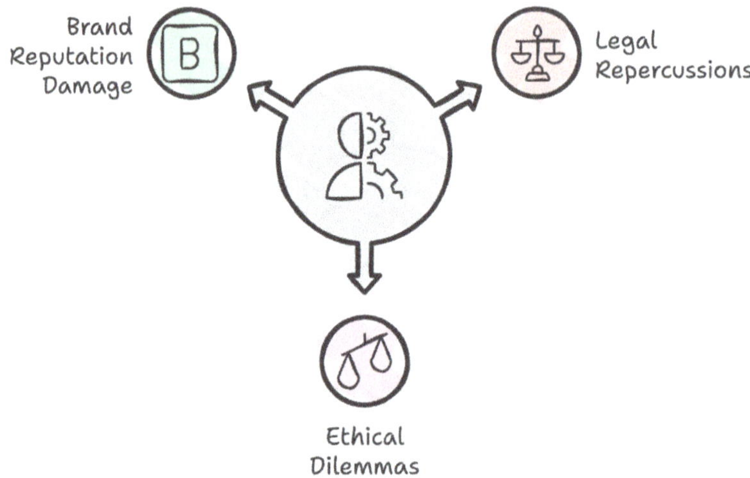

Safety constraints ensure AI outputs remain compliant with regulations and maintain brand integrity. This is particularly important in industries with strict oversight, such as finance and healthcare.

Example 1: AI in finance limits investment advice to low-risk options for novice investors.

Example 2: Customer service bots adhere to pre-approved language to maintain brand consistency.

By enforcing constraints, businesses minimize risks, maintain consistency, and uphold regulatory standards.

Bias Mitigation

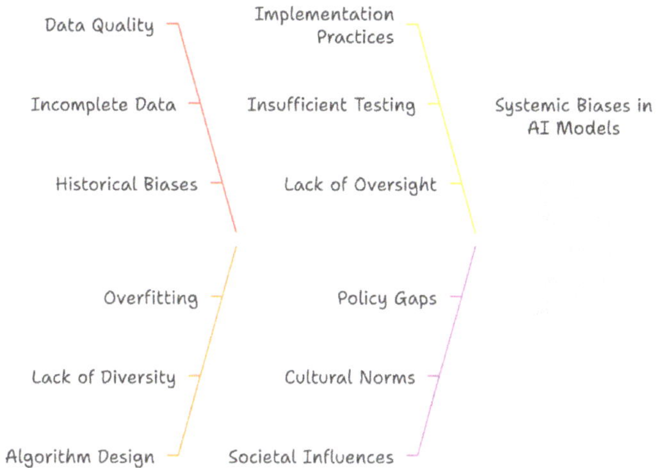

Bias mitigation involves reducing systemic biases in AI models, fostering fairness in decisions like hiring, lending, and recommendations.

Example 1: Recruitment AI is trained to avoid gender or ethnic biases, ensuring fair candidate evaluation.

Example 2: Credit scoring systems incorporate bias checks to provide equitable loan assessments across demographics.

Mitigating bias fosters fairness, compliance, and trust, particularly in sensitive applications affecting diverse user groups.

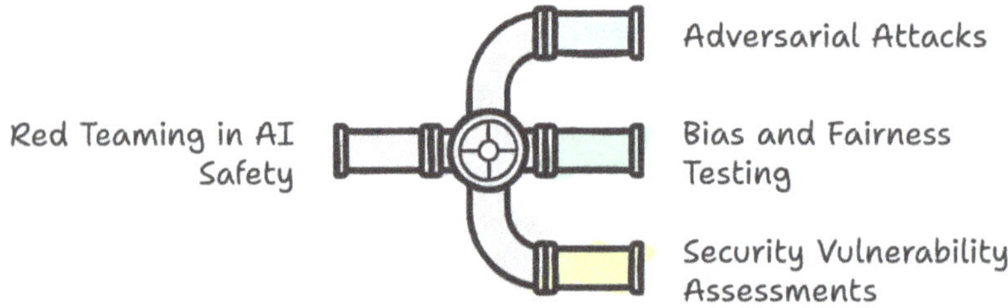

Position red teaming as a comprehensive approach to AI safety, going beyond just testing robustness. Include aspects like:

- **Adversarial Attacks:** Testing the AI's resilience against malicious inputs designed to cause it to malfunction or produce incorrect outputs.
  - **Bias and Fairness Testing:** Evaluating the AI for potential biases across different demographics and scenarios.
  - **Security Vulnerability Assessment:** Identifying potential security loopholes in the AI system that could be exploited.

Examples:

- **Social Media Platforms:** Red teaming AI algorithms to identify vulnerabilities to misinformation and hate speech.
  - **Financial Institutions:** Red teaming fraud detection systems to uncover potential weaknesses and improve their effectiveness.

- **Prompt Injection:** A technique used to manipulate or "jailbreak" AI models by carefully crafting prompts that can induce unexpected or unintended behavior.

Example: By carefully crafting a prompt, users can sometimes trick an LLM into generating inappropriate or harmful content.

Share this chapter with your team to foster a shared understanding of key concepts. Start a company-wide discussion on the potential applications of Generative AI within your organization. Attend a relevant AI conference or workshop to deepen your knowledge.

5

Transitioning from Machine Learning to Generative AI

" Machine Learning was the spark. Generative AI is the wildfire."

Sundar Pichai

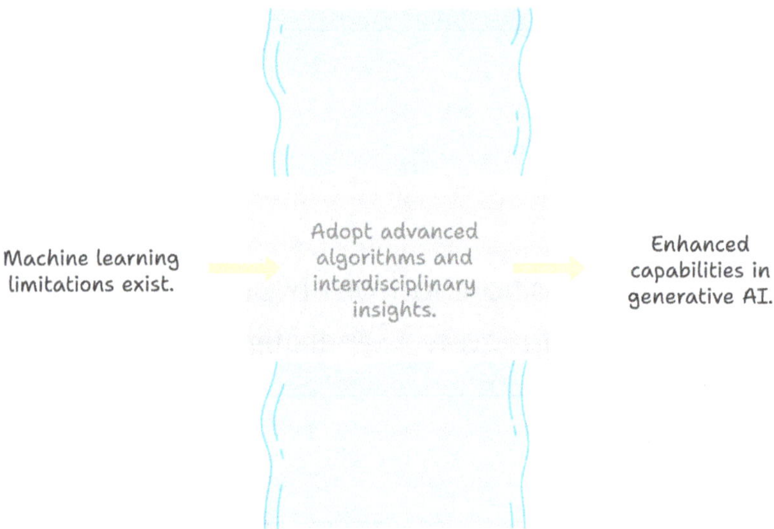

The world of Artificial Intelligence has undergone a seismic shift. Traditional Machine Learning (ML) systems, once considered the pinnacle of AI advancement, are now being complemented—and in many cases, disrupted—by Generative AI. While ML excels at prediction and classification, Generative AI takes innovation a step further, creating entirely new content, designs, and solutions.

For tech leaders, data science managers, and AI strategists, the question isn't whether to adopt Generative AI—it's how to transition seamlessly from existing ML pipelines to systems that can harness the creative power of Generative AI. This chapter serves as a practical playbook for bridging that gap, offering clarity on key differences, actionable strategies for upgrading infrastructure, and lessons from real-world transitions.

Understanding the Differences and Overlaps Between ML and Generative AI

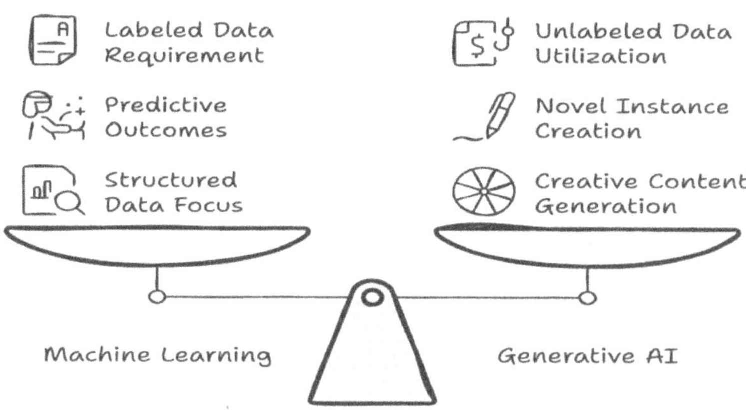

What Sets Them Apart?

While Machine Learning focuses on analyzing patterns in data to make predictions, Generative AI generates new content by learning from existing data distributions.

Aspect	Machine Learning	Generative AI
Primary Purpose	Prediction, classification	Content creation, generation
Key Algorithms	Random Forests, Gradient Boosting, Logistic Regression	Transformer Models (e.g., GPT, BERT), Diffusion Models
Input/Output	Input data ? prediction	Input data ? novel output
Example	Predicting customer churn	Generating marketing copy

Where Do They Overlap?

- **Data Dependency:** Both rely on high-quality, well-structured data.
- **Model Training:** Both require training on large datasets and validation pipelines.
- **Business Goals:** Both aim to optimize processes, reduce costs, and improve outcomes.

Practical Insight: Most of the retail company using ML for demand forecasting can layer Generative AI on top to generate personalized marketing campaigns based on forecast insights.

Why Transition Matters: Opportunities with Generative AI

Generative AI doesn't replace ML; it builds upon it. The true power lies in integrating Generative AI capabilities into existing ML pipelines.

Opportunities Enabled by Generative AI:

- **Enhanced Customer Personalization:** ML predicts user behavior; Generative AI crafts personalized responses.
- **Automated Creative Processes:** Move from data-driven insights to AI-generated content, designs, and recommendations.
- **Dynamic Decision-Making:** Combine ML predictions with Generative AI's ability to simulate multiple scenarios.

Upgrading ML Pipelines for Generative AI Integration

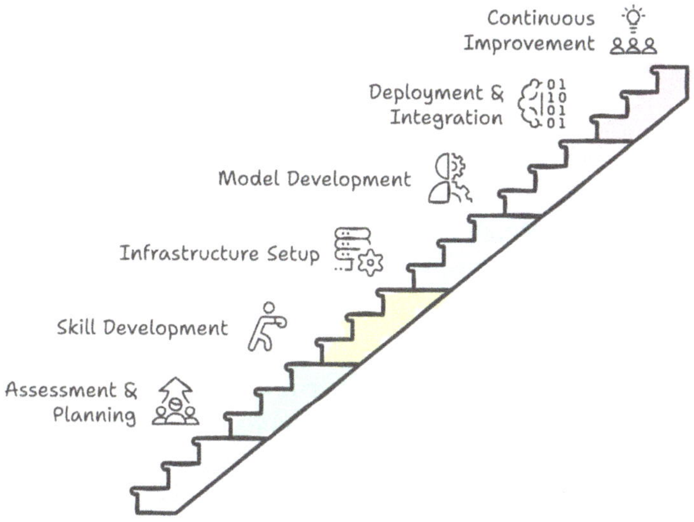

Step 1: Assess Existing ML Infrastructure

Evaluate current ML models, data pipelines, and deployment frameworks.

- Are your pipelines scalable for larger models (e.g., GPT-like architectures)?
- Do you have GPU/TPU resources for intensive training tasks?

Actionable Tip: Conduct an AI Infrastructure Audit to determine if current hardware, software, and workflows can support Generative AI workloads.

Step 2: Adopt Hybrid Models

Generative AI doesn't need to replace ML entirely. Hybrid models leverage both:

- **ML for Predictions:** E.g., customer behavior analytics.
- **Generative AI for Outputs:** E.g., personalized product recommendations.

Example Workflow:

- **ML Model:** Predict product demand for the next quarter.
- **Generative AI:** Generate promotional emails tailored to the forecasted product demand trends.

Step 3: Transition from Static to Dynamic Pipelines

- Enable **Continuous Integration/Continuous Deployment (CI/CD)** practices for AI.
- Build modular pipelines where ML and Generative AI components can interact seamlessly.
- Implement real-time monitoring for drift detection and error correction.

Tool Recommendations:

- **MLFlow:** For tracking and managing ML/AI experiments.
- **LangChain:** For building applications that combine ML predictions with Generative AI content.

Step 4: Fine-Tune Generative AI Models

Use your organization-specific data to fine-tune pre-trained Generative AI models (e.g., OpenAI's GPT or Anthropic's Claude).

Key Consideration: Protect proprietary data during model fine-tuning.

Practical Strategies for Implementation

Strategies for Successful AI Adoption in Organizations

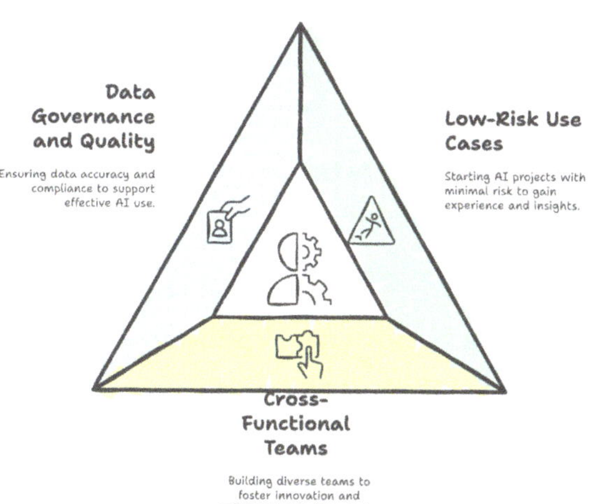

Strategy 1: Start with Low-Risk Use Cases

Begin integration with use cases where outcomes are easy to measure:

- Customer service chatbots
- Automated content creation for marketing
- Product recommendation enhancements

Example:

A retail brand starts with ML to predict seasonal trends, then applies Generative AI to automatically generate ad copy and email campaigns tailored to those predictions.

Strategy 2: Build Cross-Functional Teams
AI transitions require collaboration between:

- Data scientists
- DevOps engineers
- Product managers
- Domain experts

Create dedicated AI Transition Teams responsible for managing ML-to-Generative AI upgrades.

Strategy 3: Invest in Data Governance and Quality
Generative AI models are more sensitive to data biases and inconsistencies. Implement:

- **Robust Data Validation Pipelines**
- **Ethical AI Frameworks**

Example:JPMorgan Chase uses strict data quality pipelines when fine-tuning their AI risk management models.

A Case Study of Successful Transitions

Case Study : Traditional ML Vs. AI Models Solving Trust Deficit

Business Scenario: Credit Risk Modeling in Finance
Imagine a credit risk team at a financial institution tasked with predicting the risk score for **non-first payment default (Non-FPD)**.

Traditional Approach:

- Used **Gradient Boosting Machines (GBMs)** to build predictive models.
- Delivered **risk scores** without detailed reasoning for individual predictions.

Challenges:

- Business leaders couldn't justify decisions based on risk scores.
- Auditors questioned model transparency and compliance standards.
- Modelers struggled to explain counterintuitive predictions.

The Generative AI Solution: Enhancing Explainability

The team augmented their workflow with **Generative AI-powered Explainable AI (XAI)** models.

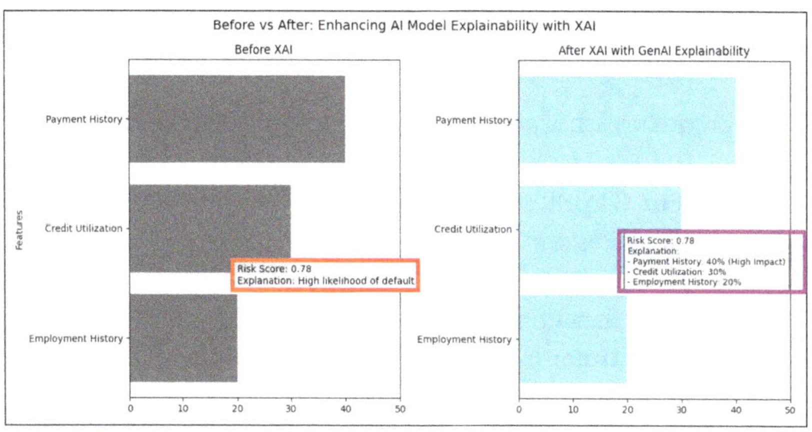

Before GenAI:

- Model Output: Risk Score = 0.78
- Explanation: "High likelihood of non-first payment default."

After GenAI:

- Model Output: Risk Score = 0.78
- Explanation:
    - **Payment history:** 40% impact (negative)
    - **Credit utilization:** 30% impact (negative)
    - **Employment history:** 20% impact (stabilizing)
- Narrative: "The high risk score is primarily due to recent missed payments (40%) and high credit utilization (30%). Employment history (20%) provided some stability."

Outcome:

- Improved transparency and trust with stakeholders.
- Faster approvals from auditors.
- Clear narratives for decision-makers.

Overcoming Challenges in Transitioning to Generative AI

- **Talent Gap:** Upskill ML teams on Generative AI architectures and tools.
- **Cost Management:** Optimize resource-heavy models for cost-efficient deployment.
- **Governance:** Implement AI ethics committees to monitor Generative AI outputs.

Pro Tip: Leverage **AI-as-a-Service (AIaaS)** platforms like AWS Bedrock and Azure OpenAI Service to reduce infrastructure costs and operational complexity.

Measuring Success in the Transition

Transitioning from ML to Generative AI requires clear Key Performance Indicators (KPIs) to track progress and measure ROI.

Key Metrics to Monitor:

- **Performance Improvements:**Accuracy of predictions vs. quality of generated content.
- **Cost Efficiency:**Reduction in operational and deployment costs.
- **Speed of Deployment:**Time taken to roll out new Generative AI models.
- **User Engagement Metrics:**Increase in click-through rates, conversions, or user satisfaction scores.

Example Dashboard:

Metric	Pre-Transition (ML Only)	Post-Transition (ML + Generative AI)
Email Engagement	15%	27%
Design Turnaround	72 hours	24 hours
Content Accuracy	85%	92%

Actionable Tip: Set up AI dashboards using tools like Tableau or Power BI to visualize progress in real time.

Future-Proofing Your AI Infrastructure

The integration of Machine Learning and Generative AI presents exciting opportunities for innovation across multiple fields. Implementing generative models (e.g., GANs, VAEs) to create new checkpoints to enhance the training dataset, simulate scenarios, and enhance outputs.

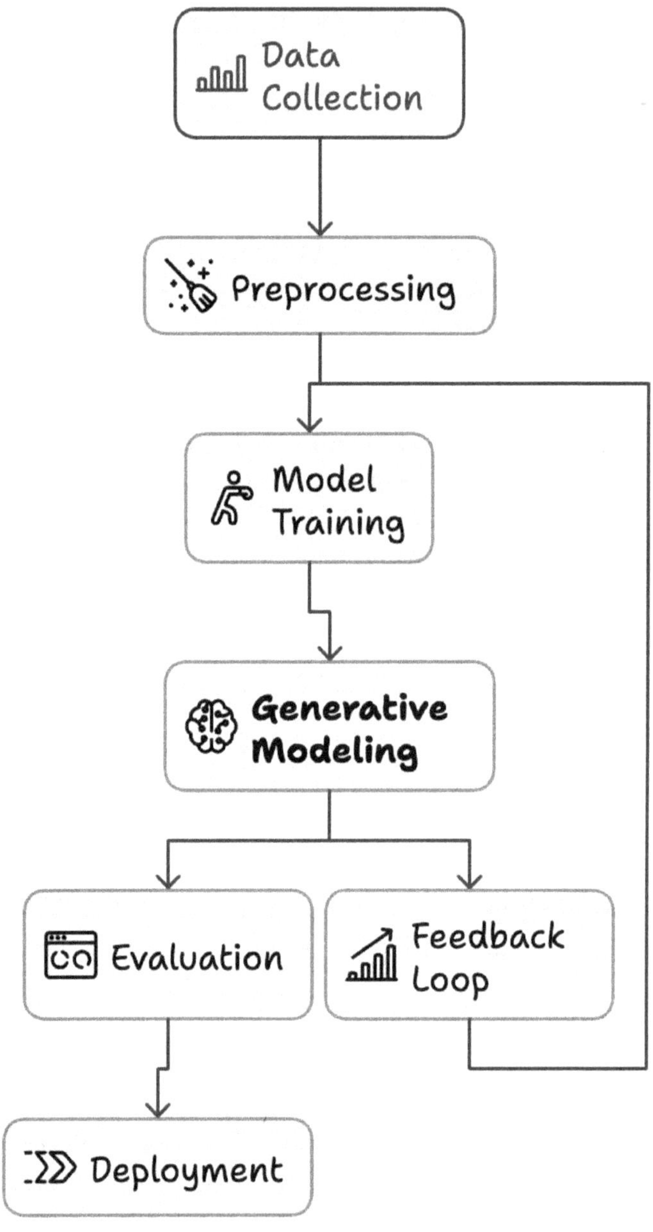
Hybrid ML Workflow
Data Collection
Preprocessing
Model Training
Generative Modeling
Evaluation
Feedback Loop
Deployment

Generative AI is not static; it's evolving rapidly. Organizations must prepare for the next wave of advancements:

- **Scalable Infrastructure:** Cloud-native architectures for AI workloads.
- **Open-Source Adoption:** Tools like Hugging Face, LangChain, and PyTorch for customization.
- **Continuous Learning:** Regular retraining and fine-tuning of models.
- **AI Governance Frameworks:** Transparent monitoring and control mechanisms.

Insight from Google DeepMind: Companies that combine ML's analytical power with Generative AI's creative capabilities are **2.3x** more likely to achieve measurable business impact.

Transitioning from Machine Learning to Generative AI isn't a one-time project—it's an ongoing transformation. It's about blending predictive power with creative potential, upgrading infrastructure, and building teams ready to harness the next wave of AI advancements.

Whether you're starting small or aiming for enterprise-wide AI integration, this chapter equips you with the strategies, insights, and practical guidance to bridge the gap confidently.

6

AI in Action – Proven Use Cases Driving Business Success

"Talk is cheap. Show me the code."

Linus Torvalds

Artificial Intelligence (AI) has transitioned from being a futuristic buzzword to an essential tool driving tangible results across industries. However, the true power of AI lies in its ability to **solve real-world problems** with measurable outcomes. Whether it's increasing sales through hyper-personalization, optimizing backend logistics, or enhancing customer support through intelligent automation, AI is redefining business strategies at every level.

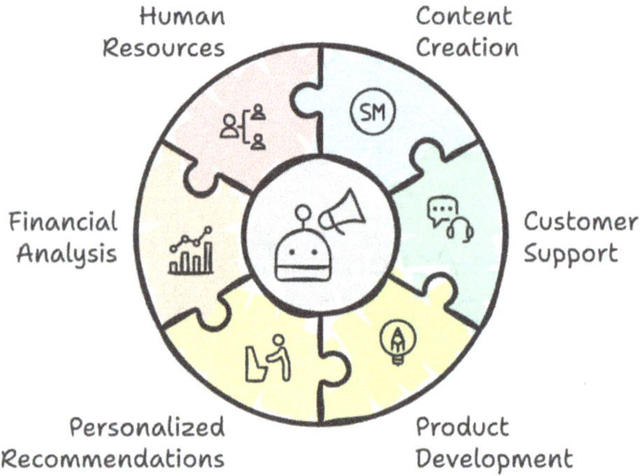

This chapter explores specific **AI use cases**, each designed to address a critical business challenge. From personalized marketing campaigns to predictive maintenance and fraud detection, every example is backed by a practical **Python code snippet** to illustrate implementation. These use cases will not only demonstrate how AI works but also why it matters to your organization.

The upcoming sections include actionable insights, real-world data-driven examples, and architectural diagrams to simplify complex concepts.

Credit Card Recommendation

In an era where customers expect tailored experiences, personalization has become the golden key to increasing conversions and improving loyalty. AI excels at analyzing patterns, predicting preferences, and delivering highly customized recommendations at scale.

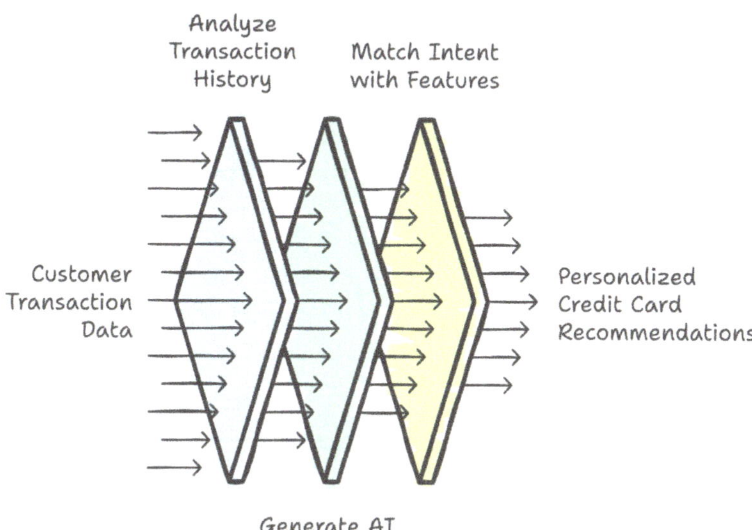

Business Scenario: Credit Card Recommendations

Imagine a scenario where:

- A customer's **transaction history** is analyzed to uncover spending behavior.
- Each credit card is represented by an **AI-generated embedding** capturing its unique benefits.
- An **AI model** matches customer intent with credit card features, ranking them in order of relevance.

This level of personalization not only drives engagement but also directly impacts revenue.

Python Implementation: Personalized Credit Card Recommendations

Below is an example of how **Generative AI models** (like GPT and BERT) can drive personalized recommendations for financial products.

Step 1: Import Required Libraries
====================================

```
import pandas as pd
import openai
from transformers import AutoTokenizer, AutoModel
import torch
```

====================================
Step 2: Load and Prepare Data
====================================

```
# Load customer and transaction data
customer_data = pd.read_csv('customer_data.csv')
transaction_data = pd.read_csv('transaction_data.csv')

# Handle missing demographic values
customer_data['age'] =
customer_data['age'].fillna(customer_data['age'].median())
customer_data['income'] =
customer_data['income'].fillna(customer_data['income'].media
n())

# Aggregate transaction summaries
transaction_summaries =
transaction_data.groupby('customer_id')['transaction_descrip
tion'].apply(lambda x: ' '.join(x))
```

==================================

Step 3: Generate Embeddings Using BERT

==================================

```
# Load pre-trained BERT model
tokenizer = AutoTokenizer.from_pretrained("bert-base-
uncased")
model = AutoModel.from_pretrained("bert-base-uncased")

# Function to generate embeddings
def generate_embeddings(text_list):
    """
    Generate embeddings using a pre-trained BERT model.
    """
    inputs = tokenizer(text_list, padding=True,
truncation=True, return_tensors="pt")
    with torch.no_grad():
        outputs = model(**inputs)
        embeddings = outputs.last_hidden_state.mean(dim=1)
    return embeddings

# Generate embeddings for transactions and credit cards
transaction_embeddings =
generate_embeddings(transaction_summaries.tolist())
credit_card_data = pd.read_csv('credit_card_data.csv')
credit_card_descriptions =
credit_card_data['description'].tolist()
credit_card_embeddings =
generate_embeddings(credit_card_descriptions)
```

=====================================

Step 4: Extract Spending Intent Using GPT

=====================================

```
# Set OpenAI API key
openai.api_key = 'your_openai_api_key'

# Function for intent extraction
def extract_intent(summary):
    """
    Extract spending preferences using GPT.
    """
    prompt = f"Identify spending preferences based on this
summary: '{summary}'"
    response = openai.Completion.create(engine="text-
davinci-003", prompt=prompt, max_tokens=50)
    return response['choices'][0]['text'].strip()

# Apply intent extraction
customer_data['spending_intent'] =
transaction_summaries.apply(extract_intent)
```

====================================

Step 5: Recommend Credit Cards Using GPT

====================================

```
# Function for credit card recommendation
def recommend_credit_card(intent, card_descriptions):
    """
    Recommend credit cards based on spending intent.
    """
    prompt = f"Recommend top 3 credit cards for a customer
with spending preferences: {intent} from these options:
{card_descriptions}"
    response = openai.Completion.create(engine="text-
davinci-003", prompt=prompt, max_tokens=100)
    return response['choices'][0]['text'].strip()

# Generate recommendations
customer_data['recommended_cards'] =
customer_data['spending_intent'].apply(
    lambda intent: recommend_credit_card(intent,
credit_card_descriptions)
)
```

====================================

Step 6: Display Recommendations

====================================

```
# Display personalized credit card recommendations for a
customer
customer_id = 12345
recommended_cards =
customer_data.loc[customer_data['customer_id'] ==
customer_id, 'recommended_cards'].values[0]
print(f"Recommended credit cards for customer {customer_id}:
{recommended_cards}")
```

====================================

Key Insights and ROI Impact

Personalized Credit Card Recommendationsleverage the power of AI to deliver tailored product offerings, aligning precisely with individual customer needs and behaviors. By analyzing transaction histories and extracting spending intent dynamically, this use case demonstrates how businesses can enhance customer experience and drive revenue growth.

Key Insights and ROI Impact

1. **Hyper-Personalization at Scale**: AI systems analyze detailed customer data, such as transaction history, spending categories, and lifestyle preferences, to recommend the most relevant credit cards. For example, a customer frequently dining at restaurants may be offered a card with high cashback on dining.
2. **Dynamic Adaptation with GPT Models**: Using generative AI models like GPT, customer spending intent is extracted dynamically. This ensures recommendations are contextually accurate and evolve with changing customer behaviors, such as shifting priorities during holiday seasons or economic downturns.
3. **Scalability and Automation**: The AI-driven system can handle millions of customer profiles with minimal human intervention, enabling financial institutions to personalize marketing efforts at scale without significantly increasing operational costs.
4. **Real-World ROI Example**

A leading financial institution faced challenges in upselling credit cards despite robust marketing campaigns. The issue stemmed from generic offers that failed to resonate with customers' unique spending patterns.

Solution: The company deployed an AI-powered recommendation engine that leveraged transaction data and generative AI to understand spending intent. This enabled the bank to deliver personalized credit card recommendations directly through email, app notifications, and website banners.

Results:

- Conversion rates improved from **12% to 20%**, surpassing industry benchmarks.
- Revenue from credit card sign-ups increased by an additional **$1.5 million per quarter**.
- Customer satisfaction scores rose by **18%**, as tailored offerings aligned with individual needs, fostering loyalty.

Example in Action: A frequent traveler was recommended a co-branded airline credit card with high rewards on flights and lounge access, increasing the likelihood of application. Similarly, a young professional with high e-commerce spending was offered a cashback card tailored for online shopping.

Further Reading: For insights into how AI is transforming credit card personalization, explore case studies and tools from companies like **Visa**(https://usa.visa.com/), which highlight successful AI-driven initiatives in financial services.

By embedding AI into the credit card recommendation process, businesses can not only enhance customer experience but also achieve measurable financial gains, positioning themselves as leaders in a competitive market.

AI Powered Precision Marketing Campaigns for Telecom

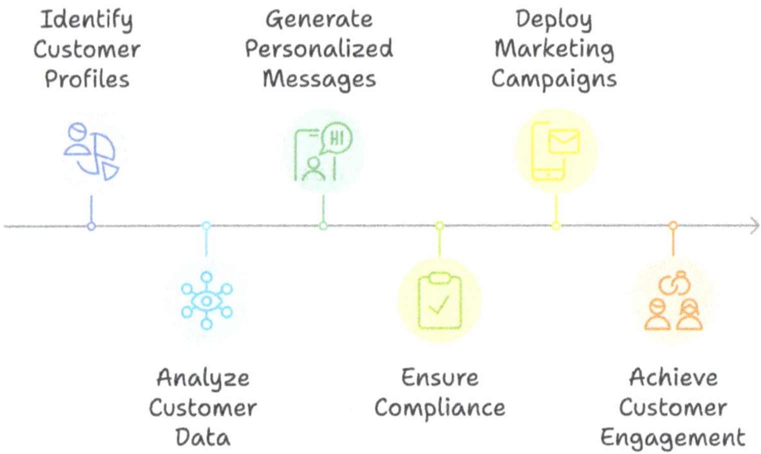

In the highly competitive telecom industry, customer engagement hinges on the ability to deliver hyper-personalized marketing messages across diverse digital platforms. Generic campaigns often fail to capture attention or drive conversions, while overly broad targeting wastes resources. Generative AI offers a transformative approach to creating dynamic, **context-aware campaigns** tailored to individual preferences, usage patterns, and service plans.

By integrating **intent extraction**, **guardrails for content quality**, and **AI-driven personalization**, telecom companies can create messaging that feels intuitive, relevant, and human-like. Whether it's a data-hungry college student receiving an SMS about unlimited streaming options or a frequent international caller getting an email about discounted rates, the result is stronger engagement and higher revenue generation.

Business Scenario: Precision Marketing with AI in Telecom

Imagine this scenario:

1. A customer frequently streams high-definition videos on their mobile plan.
2. Another customer makes frequent international calls.
3. A third prefers to communicate via social media rather than email or SMS.

Generative AI evaluates demographic data, usage behavior, and communication channel preferences to:

- **Craft context-aware marketing messages** tailored to the individual.
- **Apply guardrails** to ensure content adheres to regulatory, ethical, and brand guidelines.
- **Deploy campaigns dynamically** across SMS, email, or social platforms, maximizing reach and relevance.

Python Implementation: Generative AI-Driven Marketing Campaigns

Below is an example of how **Generative AI models** (like GPT) can be integrated into a marketing pipeline for telecom campaigns, ensuring tailored content with built-in guardrails.

Step 1: Import Required Libraries
==================================

```
import pandas as pd
import openai
import re
```

==================================

Step 2: Sample Customer Data

==

```
# Sample dataset representing telecom customer segments
data = {
    "customer_id": [101, 102, 103],
    "age_group": ["18-24", "25-34", "35-44"],
    "usage_pattern": ["High Data Usage", "Frequent
International Calls", "Video Streaming"],
    "current_plan": ["Basic", "International", "Premium"],
    "preferred_channel": ["Instagram", "Email", "SMS"]
}

# Convert to DataFrame
customer_data = pd.DataFrame(data)
print("Sample Customer Data:")
print(customer_data)
```

==

Step 3: Define Guardrails for Content Validation

==

```
# Define banned words and content constraints
banned_words = ["cheap", "unlimited free", "explicit",
"offensive"]

# Validation function for content guardrails
def validate_message(message):
    """
    Validates the marketing message against guardrails.
    """
    # Length Check
    if len(message) > 200:
        print("Message too long. Trimming to 200
characters.")
        message = message[:197] + "..."

    # Banned Words Check
    if any(word in message.lower() for word in
banned_words):
        print("Message contains banned words. Flagging for
review.")
        return "Content does not meet guardrail standards.
Please regenerate."

    # Misleading Language Check
    if re.search(r"\bunlimited\b|\bfree\b", message,
re.IGNORECASE):
        print("Message contains potentially misleading
terms.")
        return "Content does not meet guardrail standards.
Please regenerate."

    return message
```

==

Step 4: Generate Marketing Messages Using GPT

==

```
# Set OpenAI API Key
openai.api_key = 'your_openai_api_key'

# Function to generate AI marketing message
def generate_marketing_message(age_group, usage_pattern,
current_plan, channel):
    """
    Generate marketing message tailored to customer segment
using GPT.
    """
    prompt = (
        f"Create a professional, engaging telecom marketing
message for a {age_group} customer "
        f"with {usage_pattern} who is on a {current_plan}
plan. The message should be suitable for {channel}."
    )

    response = openai.Completion.create(
        engine="text-davinci-003",
        prompt=prompt,
        max_tokens=100,
        temperature=0.7
    )
    message = response['choices'][0]['text'].strip()

    # Apply guardrails
    return validate_message(message)
```

==================================

Step 5: Apply AI-Generated Campaigns to Customer Data

==================================

```
# Generate marketing messages for each customer
customer_data['marketing_message'] = customer_data.apply(
    lambda row: generate_marketing_message(
        row['age_group'], row['usage_pattern'],
row['current_plan'], row['preferred_channel']
    ),
    axis=1
)

# Display results
print("\nGenerated Marketing Messages:")
print(customer_data[['customer_id', 'marketing_message']])
```

==================================

Example Output

==================================

Customer ID	Marketing Message
101	"Enjoy uninterrupted streaming with our Premium Plan upgrade. Get more data and zero buffering!"
102	"Stay connected with family overseas. Switch to our International Plan for better rates!"
103	"Upgrade now for exclusive discounts on your next recharge!"

==================================

If a message violates a guardrail:

==================================

Customer ID	Marketing Message
102	"Content does not meet guardrail standards. Please regenerate."

==================================

Key Insights and ROI Impact

AI-Powered Precision Marketing Campaigns for Telecom utilize advanced AI capabilities to deliver highly targeted and relevant messaging, optimizing customer engagement and driving revenue. By analyzing customer usage patterns, demographics, and preferences, telecom companies can craft tailored campaigns that resonate with diverse customer segments.

1. **Targeted Messaging at Scale**: AI models analyze vast datasets, such as call patterns, data usage, and customer demographics, to segment audiences effectively. For instance, a customer with high data usage might receive offers for unlimited data plans, while international callers might be targeted with discounted roaming packages.
2. **Dynamic Personalization with Generative AI**: Generative AI models like GPT create personalized marketing messages tailored to customer needs, ensuring campaigns are engaging and relevant. For example, GPT can craft unique SMS or email content highlighting benefits specific to a customer's profile.
3. **Real-Time Adaptation**: AI systems dynamically adapt to real-time changes in customer behavior, such as increased streaming during holidays or higher roaming during travel seasons. This ensures marketing efforts remain timely and effective.
4. **Real-World ROI Example**

A leading telecom provider faced stagnant engagement rates in its marketing campaigns due to generic, one-size-fits-all messaging. Customers were often inundated with irrelevant promotions, leading to low conversion rates.

Solution: The company implemented an AI-driven precision marketing system that analyzed customer behavior and preferences. Generative AI was used to craft personalized content for each segment and deliver it through the customer's preferred communication channel, such as SMS, email, or in-app notifications.

Results:

- Campaign engagement rates increased by **30%**, as personalized messages resonated with customer needs.
- Offer redemption rates improved from **8% to 15%**, leading to a **$2 million revenue boost per quarter**.
- Customer churn reduced by **12%**, as targeted offers enhanced loyalty and satisfaction.

Example in Action:

- A young professional with high mobile data usage received an exclusive upgrade offer for an unlimited data plan with free video streaming subscriptions.
- A frequent traveler was targeted with roaming discounts via SMS as soon as they arrived in a new country, enhancing their experience while abroad.

Further Reading: Learn how companies like T-Mobile and Verizon are leveraging AI to create hyper-targeted marketing campaigns that improve engagement and ROI.

By integrating AI-powered precision marketing, telecom companies can optimize their outreach strategies, improve customer engagement, and achieve significant financial gains, all while building stronger, more personalized customer relationships.

AI Chatbot for Banking & Finance Customer Support

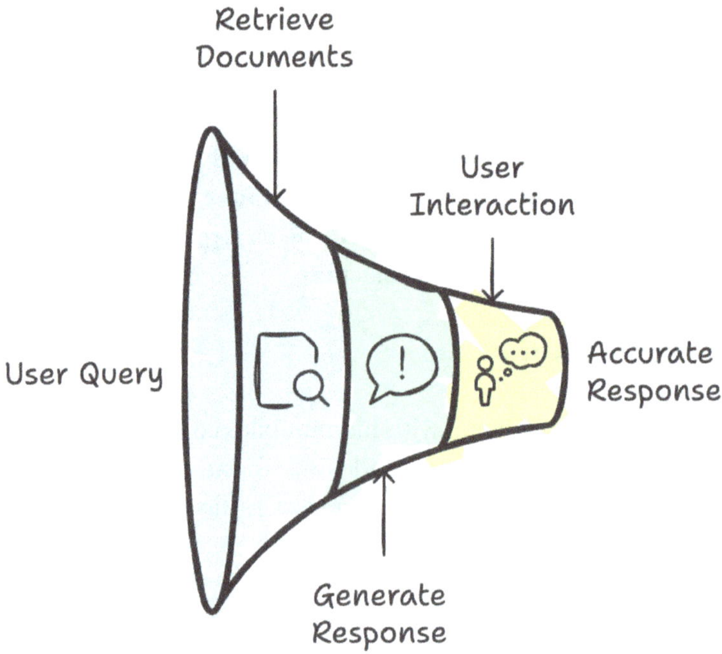

In the fast-paced world of **banking and finance**, timely and accurate customer support is non-negotiable. Customers expect **24/7 availability**, **instant responses**, and **personalized assistance** across digital channels. Traditional customer service models, reliant on human agents alone, often struggle to meet these demands efficiently, leading to **long wait times**, **operational bottlenecks**, and **escalating costs**.

Generative AI chatbots powered by **Retrieval-Augmented**

Generation (RAG) have emerged as a transformative solution. By combining **information retrieval from structured knowledge bases** with **generative AI for contextual conversation**, these chatbots can handle **routine inquiries**, **policy clarifications**, and even **personalized financial advice** with unmatched precision and scalability.

Business Scenario: Intelligent Banking Chatbot Assistance

Imagine a customer-facing scenario at a leading financial institution:

1. A customer asks, "How do I reset my online banking password?"
2. Another queries, "What are the steps to file an insurance claim?"
3. A third wants to know, "Which credit card offers the best cashback rewards for dining?"

Generative AI chatbots using **RAG pipelines** can:

- **Instantly retrieve relevant information** from a pre-built knowledge base.
- **Understand the user's intent** and **contextually respond** in a conversational style.
- **Refine answers dynamically** based on follow-up questions or clarifications.

This hybrid approach ensures **accurate responses** while preserving a **human-like interaction style**, leading to **improved customer satisfaction**, **cost efficiency**, and **scalable operations**.

RAG in Banking & Finance Chatbots

At the core of this intelligent chatbot system is **Retrieval-Augmented Generation (RAG)** — an AI architecture that bridges the gap between **static knowledge repositories** and **dynamic generative models**.

- **Retrieval:**The chatbot retrieves precise answers from a **pre-structured database** using **document search techniques** like **TF-IDF** or **vector similarity search**.
- **Augmentation:**The retrieved answer serves as a **contextual guide** for a **generative model (e.g., GPT-3)** to produce a **human-like response** tailored to the query.

This two-step approach ensures that the chatbot's answers are **factually accurate** and **contextually rich**, avoiding common issues like **hallucinations** (fabricated AI responses).

Python Implementation: RAG-Based Generative AI Chatbot

Below is a Python pipeline showcasing how **RAG (Retrieval-Augmented Generation)** can power customer support chatbots in banking and finance.

Step 1: Import Required Libraries

==

```
import pandas as pd
import openai
from sklearn.feature_extraction.text import TfidfVectorizer
from sklearn.metrics.pairwise import cosine_similarity
```

==

Step 2: Build a Knowledge Base
====================================

```
# Simulated Knowledge Base for Banking & Insurance FAQs
data = {
    "question": [
        "How do I open a new bank account?",
        "What is the process for filing an insurance
claim?",
        "How can I apply for a credit card?",
        "What are the different types of insurance
policies?",
        "How to reset my online banking password?"
    ],
    "answer": [
        "Visit our branch with a government-issued ID and
proof of address to open an account.",
        "Log in to your account, navigate to 'Claims' and
follow the instructions.",
        "Fill out an online application form or visit a
branch to apply for a credit card.",
        "We offer health, life, car, and property insurance
policies.",
        "Go to the login page, click on 'Forgot Password',
and follow the steps."
    ]
}

# Create a DataFrame
knowledge_base = pd.DataFrame(data)
print("Knowledge Base:")
print(knowledge_base)
```

====================================

Step 3: Document Retrieval Using TF-IDF
====================================

```
# Initialize TF-IDF Vectorizer
vectorizer = TfidfVectorizer()
tfidf_matrix =
vectorizer.fit_transform(knowledge_base['answer'])
```

==

Step 4: Retrieval-Augmented Generation Function

==

```
# OpenAI API Key
openai.api_key = 'your_openai_api_key'

def retrieve_and_generate_response(query):
    """
    Retrieve relevant answers from the knowledge base and
generate a conversational response.
    """
    # Step 1: Retrieve the Most Relevant Document
    query_vector = vectorizer.transform([query])
    similarity_scores = cosine_similarity(query_vector,
tfidf_matrix)
    best_match_idx = similarity_scores.argmax()
    retrieved_answer =
knowledge_base.iloc[best_match_idx]['answer']
    print(f"Retrieved Answer: {retrieved_answer}")

    # Step 2: Generate a Conversational Response Using GPT
    prompt = (
        f"Customer Query: '{query}'\n"
        f"Knowledge Base Answer: '{retrieved_answer}'\n"
        f"Generate a conversational and helpful response
based on this information."
    )

    response = openai.Completion.create(
        engine="text-davinci-003",
        prompt=prompt,
        max_tokens=100,
        temperature=0.7
    )

    return response['choices'][0]['text'].strip()
```

=======================================

Step 5: Example Queries and Responses

=======================================

```
# Sample Customer Queries
queries = [
    "How do I reset my online banking password?",
    "I want to apply for a credit card.",
    "What types of insurance do you offer?"
]

# Generate Responses for Queries
for query in queries:
    response = retrieve_and_generate_response(query)
    print(f"\nCustomer Query: {query}")
    print(f"Chatbot Response: {response}")
```

=======================================

Example Output

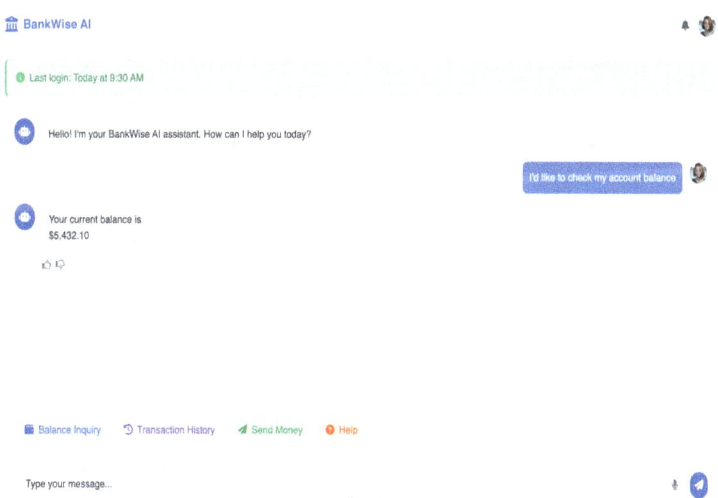

Key Insight and ROI Impact

AI chatbots have revolutionized customer support in the banking and finance sector by providing instant, accurate, and scalable assistance. Leveraging Generative AI, these chatbots can understand complex queries, offer personalized guidance, and ensure seamless customer experiences across multiple channels.

1. **Instant Assistance and Scalability**: AI chatbots operate 24/7, providing instant responses to customer queries, ranging from account balances to loan applications. This reduces customer wait times and eliminates reliance on manual support during peak hours.
2. **Cost Efficiency**: By automating repetitive tasks like answering FAQs, AI chatbots free up human agents to focus on high-value, complex queries. This reduces operational costs significantly.
3. **Enhanced Personalization**: Generative AI allows chatbots to deliver context-aware, personalized responses based on customer profiles and histories. For example, a chatbot can recommend investment products tailored to a customer's financial goals.
4. **Compliance and Accuracy**: With built-in regulatory guardrails, AI chatbots ensure responses are compliant with financial regulations, minimizing the risk of errors or misinformation.
5. **Real-World ROI Example**

A multinational bank struggled with high call center costs and inconsistent customer support experiences. Customers frequently faced long wait times for basic inquiries, leading to dissatisfaction and lost business opportunities.

Solution: The bank deployed an AI-powered chatbot that could handle up to 80% of customer queries, including account inquiries, transaction statuses, and mortgage eligibility. Generative

AI enhanced the chatbot's ability to understand natural language queries and provide contextually accurate responses.

Results:

- **Cost Savings**: Operational costs reduced by **$4 million annually** by automating routine queries.
- **Improved Customer Satisfaction**: The bank's Net Promoter Score (NPS) increased by **15 points**, driven by faster resolution times.
- **Scalability**: The chatbot handled over **1 million queries per month**, reducing call center workload by **60%**.
- **Increased Conversions**: Personalized product recommendations via the chatbot led to a **20% increase in loan applications**.

Example in Action:

- A customer inquiring about credit card eligibility was seamlessly guided through the application process, with the chatbot dynamically adjusting responses based on the customer's spending habits and preferences.
- A first-time investor received tailored insights about mutual fund options based on their risk tolerance, delivered through a conversational chatbot interface.

Further Reading: Explore how JPMorgan Chase's COiN platform and Bank of America's Erica are transforming customer support with AI-driven chatbots.

By adopting AI chatbots, banking and finance organizations can deliver exceptional customer support, reduce operational costs, and enhance customer engagement. These systems not only streamline customer interactions but also build trust by ensuring consistent, accurate, and personalized experiences.

As we've seen in previous use cases, **Generative AI is a**

powerful force in driving business transformation, whether it's optimizing customer experiences, automating repetitive tasks, or offering personalized insights. But one of the most impactful applications of Generative AI lies in **content creation at scale**—where AI doesn't just analyze data but generates valuable outputs such as marketing copy, educational material, customer support responses, and more.

Let's dive into our next use case, where we explore the practical implementation of **Generative AI-driven content generation through an interactive application interface**.

AI Content Generation for Personalized Messaging

In the **EdTech industry**, delivering engaging, age-specific, and platform-relevant content is vital for attracting and retaining learners. With diverse learner profiles spanning from young students to adult professionals, **one-size-fits-all content strategies fall short**.

Generative AI steps in as a game-changer by creating **hyper-personalized educational content** tailored to specific age groups, interests, and delivery platforms. This includes **social media posts**, **learning module summaries**, **interactive quizzes**, and **bite-sized educational insights** — all dynamically generated to meet the preferences of different audience segments.

But Generative AI doesn't stop at just creating content. **Content moderation** becomes equally essential to ensure the generated material aligns with **educational guidelines**, avoids bias, and meets quality standards.

In this use case, we'll explore how Generative AI can:

1. **Generate high-quality educational content** personalized for different audiences.
2. **Adapt content tone and format** based on target platforms like Instagram, Facebook, or LinkedIn.

3. **Ensure content moderation** to filter out inappropriate material and maintain educational integrity.

Business Scenario: AI-Powered Personalized Content in EdTech

Imagine this scenario:

- **Scenario 1:**A **high-school student** following STEM topics on Instagram receives **interactive posts** featuring exciting science experiments and coding bootcamp opportunities.
- **Scenario 2:**A **language-learning enthusiast** on Facebook is shown **daily language tips** paired with real-world conversation scenarios.
- **Scenario 3:**A **career-focused professional** on LinkedIn gets **personalized recommendations** for upskilling workshops and industry-relevant courses.

In each case, AI ensures that the content is **highly targeted**, **platform-optimized**, and **educationally valuable**.

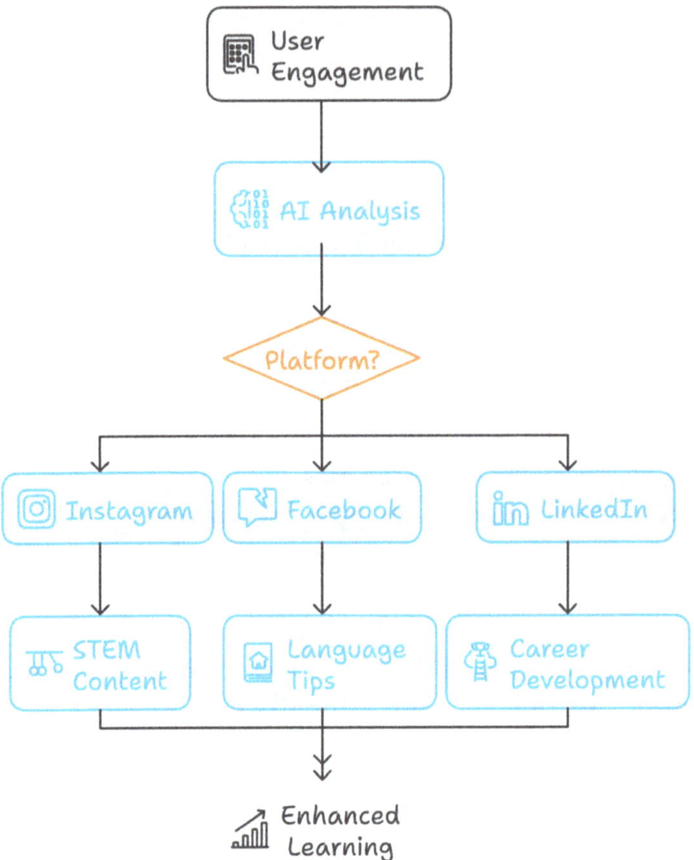

While **content generation** focuses on crafting engaging material, **content moderation** ensures that the generated posts are **relevant**, **safe**, and **compliant** with educational and platform guidelines.

For example:

1. Removing misleading phrases like "free forever" or "guaranteed results."
2. Ensuring age-appropriate content is generated for different learner groups.
3. Filtering out biased or inappropriate language.

By combining **generation** and **moderation**, EdTech platforms can deliver consistent, trustworthy, and engaging experiences to their audiences.

Python Implementation: Content Generation & Moderation for EdTech (with Streamlit UI)

Below is a **Python pipeline** that integrates Generative AI for **content generation** and **content moderation**, paired with a **Streamlit app for user interaction**.

Step 1: Install Required Libraries
====================================

```
#Make sure these libraries are installed:
pip install pandas openai streamlit
```

====================================
Step 2: Import Required Libraries
====================================

```
import pandas as pd
import openai
import streamlit as st
import re

# OpenAI API Key
openai.api_key = 'your_openai_api_key'
```

======================================

Step 3: Sample Audience Data

======================================

```
# Sample Audience Data for EdTech Marketing
data = {
    "customer_id": [1, 2, 3],
    "age_group": ["18-24", "25-34", "35-44"],
    "interests": ["STEM Education", "Language Learning",
"Career Development"],
    "preferred_platform": ["Instagram", "Facebook",
"LinkedIn"]
}

audience_data = pd.DataFrame(data)
```

====================================

Step 4: Content Generation Function with Guardrails

====================================

```
def generate_social_media_post(age_group, interests, 
platform):
    """
    Generate social media posts using GPT-3 based on 
audience preferences.
    """
    prompt = (
        f"Create an engaging educational social media post 
for an audience aged {age_group}, "
        f"interested in {interests}, and optimized for the 
{platform} platform."
    )

    response = openai.Completion.create(
        engine="text-davinci-003",
        prompt=prompt,
        max_tokens=100,
        temperature=0.7
    )

    content = response['choices'][0]['text'].strip()

    # Apply moderation guardrails
    banned_words = ["free forever", "guaranteed results", 
"explicit"]
    if any(word in content.lower() for word in 
banned_words):
        return "Content did not meet moderation standards. 
Please regenerate."

    return content
```

=======================================

Step 5: Streamlit App for User Interaction

Create a **app.py** file and add the following code:

=======================================

```
st.title("AI-Driven Educational Content Generator")

# Sidebar for input parameters
st.sidebar.header("Audience Details")
age_group = st.sidebar.selectbox("Select Age Group", ["18-
24", "25-34", "35-44"])
interests = st.sidebar.selectbox("Select Interest", ["STEM
Education", "Language Learning", "Career Development"])
platform = st.sidebar.selectbox("Select Platform",
["Instagram", "Facebook", "LinkedIn"])

# Generate content button
if st.sidebar.button("Generate Content"):
    post = generate_social_media_post(age_group, interests,
platform)
    st.write("### Generated Social Media Post:")
    st.write(post)

# Display sample dataset
st.write("### Sample Audience Data:")
st.dataframe(audience_data)
```

=======================================

Run the Streamlit app:

=======================================

```
streamlit run app.py
```

==================================

Step 6: 🖥️ Streamlit App UI Example

1. Sidebar Controls (User Input Section)

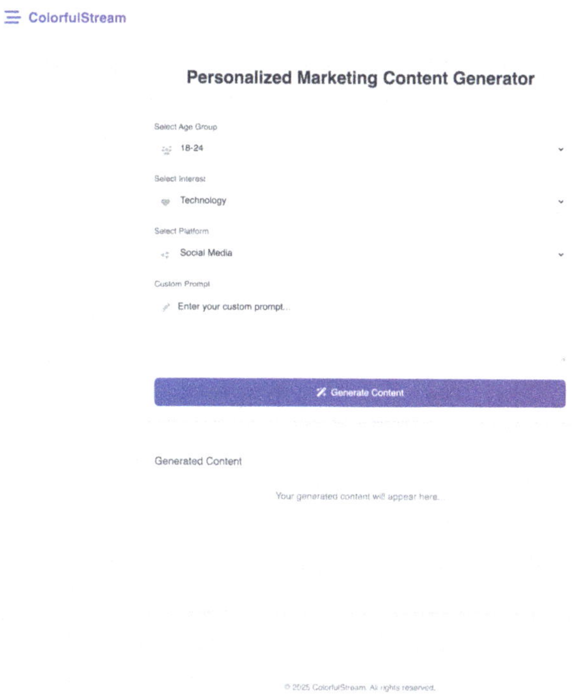

2. Main Interface

Example Generated Content:

- Instagram (18-24, STEM Education):"🚀 Dive into the world of AI and Robotics with our interactive STEM workshops! Join now and unleash your potential. #FutureTech #STEMLearning"
- LinkedIn (25-34, Career Development):"📚 Advance your career with our AI-powered leadership bootcamp. Equip yourself with future-ready skills and certifications. Sign up today!"

Key Insights and ROI Impact

AI-driven content generation has transformed personalized messaging, enabling businesses to create targeted, context-aware communication at scale. By leveraging Generative AI, organizations can deliver highly engaging messages tailored to customer preferences, behaviors, and needs, across multiple platforms like email, SMS, and social media.

1. **Dynamic Personalization**: Generative AI enables content to be customized based on customer profiles, such as purchase history, browsing behavior, and demographic data. This enhances relevance and drives higher engagement rates.
2. **Scalability and Efficiency**: Automated content generation reduces the time and resources required to create personalized messages for large customer bases, ensuring campaigns can scale seamlessly.
3. **Cross-Platform Adaptability**: AI-generated messages can be optimized for various channels, including email, SMS, push notifications, and social media, ensuring consistent brand communication.
4. **Improved Engagement and Conversion**: Tailored content resonates more deeply with customers, leading to higher open rates, click-through rates, and overall conversions.
5. **Real-World ROI Example**

An e-commerce company faced challenges with low engagement rates in its email marketing campaigns. Generic messaging failed to capture customer interest, resulting in declining sales and inefficient use of marketing budgets.

Solution: The company implemented a Generative AI platform to craft personalized email content based on individual customer preferences, browsing behavior, and purchase history. AI-generated subject lines, product recommendations, and dynamic discounts were tailored for each recipient.

Results:

- **Increased Engagement**: Email open rates improved from **12% to 25%**, and click-through rates increased by **40%**.
- **Boosted Revenue**: Personalized promotions led to a **15% uplift in sales** within three months of implementation.
- **Cost Efficiency**: The automation reduced content creation costs by **30%**, freeing up marketing teams to focus on strategy.
- **Scalable Campaigns**: The AI system generated unique messages for over **500,000 customers** weekly, ensuring timely and relevant communication.

Example in Action:

- A customer who frequently purchased fitness gear received an email with personalized recommendations for new arrivals in activewear, coupled with a limited-time discount. The email included AI-crafted headlines like "Gear Up for Your Next Adventure" and dynamic product descriptions that resonated with the customer's preferences.
- On social media, the same customer saw ads featuring workout tips and products they had previously browsed, ensuring consistent messaging across platforms.

Further Reading: Discover how AI-powered platforms like Persado and Phrasee are revolutionizing personalized marketing through content generation.

By incorporating Generative AI into content creation, businesses can elevate their messaging strategies, foster deeper connections with customers, and drive measurable outcomes. Personalized messaging powered by AI not only enhances engagement but also builds long-term loyalty by delivering value to customers at every interaction.

Generative AI for **content creation and moderation** empowers EdTech platforms to **scale content strategies**, **reduce manual overhead**, and **enhance learner engagement**. With tools like GPT and intuitive interfaces via Streamlit, the future of **AI-driven content generation & moderation** is bright, scalable, and deeply personalized.

As we've explored in previous use cases, Generative AI has proven its versatility in personalization, customer support, and content creation. However, its potential extends far beyond these realms, especially when combined with frameworks like **LangChain** for building powerful language model workflows and **Reinforcement Learning from Human Feedback (RLHF)** for fine-tuning model outputs based on human expertise.

AI Powered Compliance Automation with RLHF and LangChain

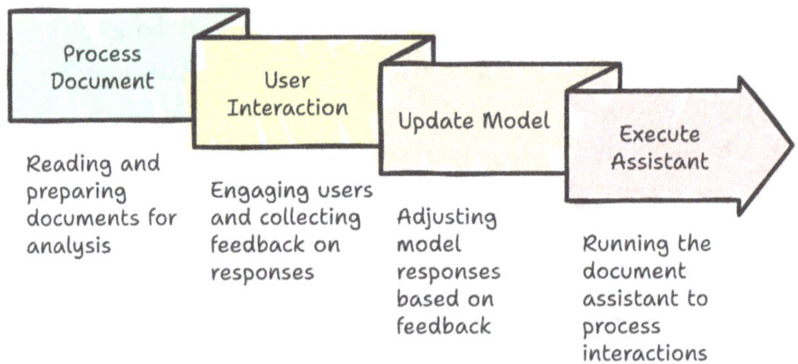

In this use case, we'll explore how organizations can leverage **LangChain** and **RLHF** to build an **Intelligent Document Assistant** — a tool designed to automate document analysis, extract key insights, and ensure compliance across regulatory-intensive industries like **Finance**, **Healthcare**, and **Legal Services**.

Business Scenario: Intelligent Document Processing for Compliance

Imagine this scenario:

- A **financial institution** processes thousands of loan applications monthly, ensuring compliance with stringent regulatory standards.
- A **healthcare organization** needs to extract critical patient information from medical records while maintaining HIPAA compliance.
- A **legal firm** must review high volumes of contracts to flag risky clauses and ensure legal compliance.

Traditionally, these tasks rely heavily on **manual review processes**, requiring teams of analysts and countless hours to extract key insights and ensure adherence to standards.

Now, imagine an **AI-powered Intelligent Document Assistant**:

- It scans documents instantly.
- Flags risks, inconsistencies, or non-compliance areas.
- Suggests actionable insights and generates compliance reports.
- Fine-tunes responses based on **human feedback (RLHF)** to ensure precision and adaptability.

This approach drastically reduces manual effort, increases efficiency, and minimizes costly compliance failures.

How RLHF and LangChain Fit In

- **RLHF (Reinforcement Learning from Human Feedback):** RLHF fine-tunes the AI model based on iterative human feedback, ensuring outputs align with real-world requirements and compliance standards.
- **LangChain:** LangChain allows the creation of sophisticated pipelines where language models can interact with external systems, retrieve documents, and execute logical workflows seamlessly.

Python Implementation: Document Assistant Using RLHF and LangChain

Below is a Python implementation that demonstrates how to build an Intelligent Document Assistant using **LangChain** for document workflows and **RLHF** for refinement.

Step 1: Install Required Libraries

=======================================

```
pip install langchain openai transformers pandas
```

=======================================

=======================================

Step 2: Import Required Libraries

=======================================

```
import os
import pandas as pd
from langchain.chains import LLMChain
from langchain.prompts import PromptTemplate
from langchain.llms import OpenAI
from transformers import pipeline
from langchain.callbacks import get_openai_callback
```

==================================

Step 3: Initialize the Environment

==================================

```
# Set OpenAI API Key
os.environ["OPENAI_API_KEY"] = "your_openai_api_key"

# Load OpenAI LLM
llm = OpenAI(temperature=0.5, model="gpt-4")
```

==================================

Step 4: Define the RLHF Refinement Function

RLHF helps refine outputs using human-labeled feedback.

```
# Simulated feedback mechanism
def rlhf_refinement(response, human_feedback):
    """
    Refines the AI response based on human feedback.
    Args:
        response: Initial AI-generated response.
        human_feedback: Human feedback on response quality.
    Returns:
        Refined response.
    """
    refinement_prompt = f"""
    Original Response: {response}
    Human Feedback: {human_feedback}

    Refine the original response based on the feedback
provided to ensure compliance and clarity.
    """
    refined_response = llm(refinement_prompt)
    return refined_response
```

==================================

Step 5: Build the Intelligent Document Workflow Using LangChain

==

```
# Define a LangChain workflow for document analysis
document_analysis_template = PromptTemplate(
    input_variables=["document_text"],
    template="""
    Analyze the following document and extract:
    - Key risks
    - Compliance violations (if any)
    - Actionable insights

    Document: {document_text}
    """
)

# Create LangChain workflow
document_chain = LLMChain(llm=llm,
prompt=document_analysis_template)

# Example Document Text
document_text = """
This loan agreement includes a variable interest rate
without a cap, which might violate regulatory guidelines.
"""

# Execute the document workflow
with get_openai_callback() as cb:
    initial_response = document_chain.run(document_text)
    print("Initial Analysis Response:")
    print(initial_response)
```

==

Step 6: Refine the Response with RLHF

==================================

```
# Simulate human feedback
human_feedback = "Highlight the regulatory risk in more
detail and suggest immediate corrective action."

# Apply RLHF for refinement
refined_response = rlhf_refinement(initial_response,
human_feedback)

print("\nRefined Response after RLHF:")
print(refined_response)
```

==================================

Step 7: Integration with External Systems (Optional)

Using LangChain's integration capabilities, responses can be logged in compliance dashboards or integrated with document management systems.

==================================

```
# Example Integration (Simulated)
compliance_report = {
    "Document": document_text,
    "Initial Analysis": initial_response,
    "Refined Analysis": refined_response
}

# Save to CSV for compliance tracking
compliance_df = pd.DataFrame([compliance_report])
compliance_df.to_csv("compliance_analysis.csv", index=False)
print("\nCompliance analysis saved to
compliance_analysis.csv")
```

==================================

Key Insights and ROI Impact

Regulatory compliance is a critical challenge for organizations across industries. Managing compliance processes manually is time-intensive, error-prone, and costly. By integrating Reinforcement Learning from Human Feedback (RLHF) and LangChain, organizations can automate compliance workflows, ensure adherence to regulations, and minimize risk.

1. **Streamlined Compliance Management**: RLHF enables AI systems to learn from human feedback, refining their ability to interpret and apply regulatory requirements accurately. This reduces the burden on compliance teams.
2. **Document Automation**: LangChain facilitates the parsing and summarization of large volumes of legal documents and policies, enabling organizations to extract actionable insights without manual intervention.
3. **Proactive Risk Mitigation**: AI can identify potential compliance risks early by monitoring internal communications, transactions, and other data streams, ensuring timely corrective actions.
4. **Scalability Across Regulations**: The solution adapts to evolving regulatory landscapes, ensuring compliance across multiple geographies and jurisdictions.
5. **Real-World ROI Example**

A multinational financial institution faced mounting challenges in complying with global anti-money laundering (AML) regulations. Manual processes for reviewing transactions and generating compliance reports led to delays and frequent errors, exposing the organization to regulatory penalties.

Solution: The institution adopted an AI-powered compliance framework leveraging RLHF and LangChain. RLHF enabled the AI model to refine its detection of suspicious activities based on expert feedback. LangChain was used to extract and summarize key clauses from AML regulations and customer onboarding documents.

Results:

- **Enhanced Efficiency**: The AI system reduced compliance review times by **70%**, enabling faster resolution of flagged cases.
- **Cost Savings**: Automation reduced operational expenses related to compliance by **40%**, saving millions annually.
- **Improved Accuracy**: False positives in transaction monitoring dropped by **30%**, allowing compliance teams to focus on genuine risks.
- **Regulatory Confidence**: Comprehensive, automated reports improved transparency during audits, reducing the likelihood of penalties.

Example in Action:

- An AI system reviewed transactions in real time, flagging anomalies like unusually large fund transfers or transactions involving high-risk countries. Alerts included summarized regulatory guidelines to assist compliance officers in decision-making.
- When onboarding a new customer, LangChain extracted essential compliance details from lengthy policy documents and generated a concise summary for the legal team, expediting the approval process.

Further Reading: Explore solutions from leaders in AI compliance like LogicGate and Trulioo for real-world applications of automated compliance workflows.

By harnessing the power of RLHF and LangChain, organizations can achieve compliance with greater speed, accuracy, and scalability. Automating these processes not only ensures regulatory adherence but also frees up resources for strategic initiatives, making compliance a competitive advantage.

Search Optimization with Vector Database and AI

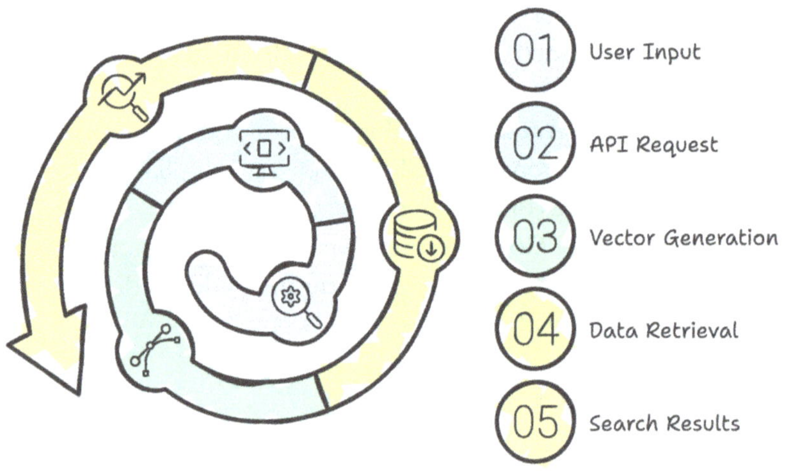

In the hospitality industry, delivering **relevant and personalized search results** is critical to driving higher bookings and enhancing the customer experience. Traditional keyword-based search engines often fail to capture **nuanced user intent**, such as preferences for specific amenities, proximity to landmarks, or budget constraints.

By combining **Generative AI** for **intent extraction** and **Vector Databases** for **semantic search**, hotel platforms can now offer highly accurate, **intent-aware search results** at scale. This approach ensures travelers find the **right hotel** faster, improving both **conversion rates** and **customer satisfaction**.

Business Scenario: Enhancing Hotel Search with Intent-Aware AI

Imagine these scenarios:

1. A **family planning a vacation** search for "kid-friendly beachfront hotel in Hawaii under $200 per night."
2. A **business traveler** looks for "hotel near downtown San Francisco with free Wi-Fi and meeting rooms."
3. A **luxury traveler** searches for "5-star resort in Bali with a spa and ocean view."

Each query is nuanced, containing **specific intents** and **preferences**. Traditional search engines might return inconsistent results, while an AI-powered search system would:

- **Extract Intent Signals:** Understand key attributes such as location, amenities, budget, and purpose of stay.
- **Match Catalog Entries:** Compare these attributes against hotel database entries using **semantic embeddings.**
- **Rank Search Results:** Prioritize hotels based on relevance, reviews, and proximity to the user's stated intent.

This results in **faster decision-making**, higher conversion rates, and an overall **enhanced booking experience**.

This use case integrates **Generative AI** with a **Vector Database** to optimize hotel search results in real-time.

- **Intent Extraction with Generative AI:** Extract user intent from free-text search queries.
- **Embedding Generation:** Convert both search queries and hotel descriptions into **vector embeddings**.

- **Semantic Search in Vector Database:** Use embeddings to perform similarity searches in a **vector database** (e.g., Pinecone, Weaviate).
- **Ranking and Scoring:** Rank results based on relevance, user preferences, and hotel-specific attributes.
- **REST API Deployment:** Expose the solution as a **scalable REST API** for seamless integration with hotel search platforms.

Technology Stack

1. **Generative AI:** OpenAI GPT for intent extraction.
2. **Vector Database:** Pinecone for scalable similarity searches.
3. **Embedding Model:** Sentence Transformers (all-MiniLM-L6-v2) for generating semantic embeddings.
4. **Frameworks:** Flask for API deployment, Pandas for data handling.

Python Implementation: AI-Powered Search API with Vector Database

Step 1: Install Required Libraries

====================================

```
pip install flask pandas openai sentence-transformers
pinecone-client
```

====================================

Step 2: Import Required Libraries

====================================

```
from flask import Flask, request, jsonify
import pandas as pd
import openai
import pinecone
from sentence_transformers import SentenceTransformer
```

====================================

Step 3: Initialize Models and Vector Database

====================================

```
# OpenAI API Key
openai.api_key = "your_openai_api_key"

# Initialize Sentence Transformer for Embeddings
embedding_model = SentenceTransformer('all-MiniLM-L6-v2')

# Initialize Pinecone Vector Database
pinecone.init(api_key="your_pinecone_api_key",
environment="gcp-starter")
index_name = "hotel-search"

# Create or connect to the Pinecone Index
if index_name not in pinecone.list_indexes():
    pinecone.create_index(index_name, dimension=384)
index = pinecone.Index(index_name)
```

====================================

Step 4: Define Intent Extraction Function

=====================================

```
def extract_intent(query):
    """
    Extract user intent from the search query using
Generative AI.
    """
    prompt = f"Extract user intent from the following hotel
search query: '{query}'"
    response = openai.Completion.create(
        engine="text-davinci-003",
        prompt=prompt,
        max_tokens=50,
        temperature=0.3
    )
    extracted_intent =
response['choices'][0]['text'].strip()
    print("Extracted Intent:", extracted_intent)
    return extracted_intent
```

=====================================

Step 5: Prepare Hotel Catalog and Upload to Pinecone

======================================

```
# Sample Hotel Catalog
hotel_catalog = pd.DataFrame({
    'hotel_id': [1, 2, 3, 4, 5],
    'name': ["Beachfront Paradise", "Downtown Business Hub",
"Luxury Spa Resort", "Family Fun Hotel", "Budget City
Stay"],
    'location': ["Hawaii", "San Francisco", "Bali",
"Orlando", "New York"],
    'amenities': ["beachfront, kid-friendly", "meeting
rooms, free Wi-Fi", "spa, ocean view", "pool, kid-friendly",
"budget-friendly"],
    'price_per_night': [200, 300, 500, 150, 100]
})

# Generate embeddings for hotel descriptions and upload to
Pinecone
for i, row in hotel_catalog.iterrows():
    description = f"{row['name']} in {row['location']} with
{row['amenities']} at ${row['price_per_night']} per night"
    embedding = embedding_model.encode(description).tolist()
    index.upsert([(str(row['hotel_id']), embedding,
row.to_dict())])
```

======================================

Step 6: Query the Vector Database

==

```
def search_hotels(user_query):
    """
    Search hotels using a query string.
    """
    # Step 1: Extract intent
    intent = extract_intent(user_query)

    # Step 2: Generate embedding for user query
    query_embedding =
embedding_model.encode(user_query).tolist()

    # Step 3: Query Pinecone for similar hotels
    search_results = index.query(
        vector=query_embedding,
        top_k=5,
        include_metadata=True
    )

    # Step 4: Format results
    results = []
    for match in search_results['matches']:
        results.append({
            'hotel_id': match['id'],
            'name': match['metadata']['name'],
            'location': match['metadata']['location'],
            'similarity_score': match['score']
        })

    return results
```

==

Step 7: Build the REST API

======================================

```
app = Flask(__name__)

@app.route('/search_hotels', methods=['POST'])
def search():
    data = request.get_json()
    query = data.get('query', '')

    # Perform search
    results = search_hotels(query)
    return jsonify(results)

if __name__ == '__main__':
    app.run(debug=True)
```

======================================

Step 8: Example API Call

======================================

```
curl -X POST -H "Content-Type: application/json" -d
'{"query": "kid-friendly beachfront hotel in Hawaii under
$200"}' http://127.0.0.1:5000/search_hotels
```

======================================

Sample Output:

======================================

```
[
    {"hotel_id": "1", "name": "Beachfront Paradise",
"location": "Hawaii", "similarity_score": 0.92},
    {"hotel_id": "4", "name": "Family Fun Hotel",
"location": "Orlando", "similarity_score": 0.85}
]
```

======================================

Key Insights and ROI Impact

In industries like e-commerce, travel, and content platforms, providing accurate and relevant search results is a game-changer for customer experience and revenue. Vector databases combined with AI models revolutionize search functionality by understanding user intent and delivering highly relevant results.

1. **Enhanced Search Precision**: Vector databases allow for similarity-based searches, enabling AI to find results that align closely with user intent rather than relying on exact keyword matches.
2. **Context-Aware Query Understanding**: AI models extract and interpret user intent from open-text search queries, ensuring the results are tailored to individual needs.
3. **Dynamic Personalization**: By incorporating user profiles, preferences, and historical data, AI can further refine search results, creating a personalized experience.
4. **Scalability for High-Volume Queries**: The integration of AI and vector databases enables platforms to handle millions of concurrent search queries without compromising accuracy or speed.
5. **Real-World ROI Example**

A leading online travel agency struggled with high bounce rates and low conversion rates due to irrelevant search results on its platform. Traditional keyword-based search often failed to understand user intent, resulting in suboptimal customer experiences.

Solution: The agency implemented an AI-powered search solution with a vector database. AI models extracted user intent from search queries (e.g., "beachfront family-friendly hotels under $200") and matched it with product embeddings stored in the vector database. The system then ranked and presented results based on relevance, user preferences, and popularity.

Results:

- **Increased Conversions**: The conversion rate improved by **15%**, resulting in an additional $5 million in quarterly revenue.
- **Reduced Bounce Rates**: Users were **20% less likely to leave the platform** after receiving more relevant search results.
- **Improved User Retention**: Personalized search experiences boosted customer retention by **10%**, fostering brand loyalty.
- **Operational Efficiency**: The vector database reduced the computational load on backend systems, cutting search query processing times by **50%**.

Example in Action:

- A user searched for **"luxury spa resorts in Europe under $500."** The AI system extracted key attributes like "**luxury**," "**spa**," "**Europe**," and "**under $500**," and mapped these to product embeddings in the vector database. Results were ranked based on similarity scores, user reviews, and popularity metrics.
- A retailer implemented the same approach for product searches, enabling users to find items visually similar to uploaded images, such as "**red sneakers with a white sole**."

Further Reading: Companies like Pinecone and Weaviate provide cutting-edge vector database solutions for scalable and efficient search optimization.

By integrating vector databases with AI, organizations can offer superior search experiences that understand user intent, adapt to their preferences, and deliver accurate results. This not only improves customer satisfaction but also drives significant business value by increasing conversions and operational efficiency.

7

AI and Cybersecurity – A Resilient Digital Future

"AI in cybersecurity is like turning the flashlight into a spotlight—illuminating threats before they become breaches."

Dr. Ian Levy

In today's hyper-connected world, cybersecurity is no longer optional—it's mission-critical. With **AI systems increasingly embedded in business operations, decision-making, and customer interactions**, safeguarding these systems against cyber threats is imperative.

But here's the catch: **AI isn't just a tool for cybersecurity—it's both a shield and a target.** While AI can predict, detect, and neutralize threats faster than traditional systems, malicious actors are also using AI to create more sophisticated attacks.

This chapter explores:

- How **AI enhances threat detection, fraud prevention, and response times**.
- The **unique vulnerabilities of AI systems** and strategies to secure them.
- Real-world examples of **AI-powered cybersecurity solutions**.
- Reflection on building a **cyber-resilient organization in an AI-first world**.

As **cyber threats evolve, so must our defenses**—and AI holds the key to building a truly resilient digital future.

The Cybersecurity Landscape: Challenges in a AI-First World

The Cybersecurity Crossroads

In an era where **every interaction, transaction, and decision leaves a digital footprint**, cybersecurity has become the backbone of sustainable digital transformation. Whether it's financial institutions safeguarding millions of transactions, e-commerce platforms protecting user data, or governments securing national infrastructure, **cyber resilience is no longer optional—it's mandatory.**

Yet, the **cyber threat landscape is evolving at breakneck speed**. As organizations embrace cloud computing, Internet of Things (IoT), remote work, and AI-powered systems, they inadvertently broaden their attack surfaces. **Threat actors are becoming more sophisticated**, leveraging AI themselves to exploit vulnerabilities and orchestrate highly targeted attacks.

This chapter explores:

- The **key cybersecurity challenges organizations face today**.
- The **rising sophistication of cyber threats** powered by AI.
- The **critical need for proactive strategies and AI-powered defenses**.
- Practical insights into building a **resilient cybersecurity ecosystem**.

The digital-first world presents both unprecedented opportunities and unparalleled risks. Let's dive into the challenges and opportunities of cybersecurity in this evolving landscape.

The Modern Cybersecurity Landscape: An Overview

1. The Expanding Attack Surface

As businesses scale digitally, the attack surface grows exponentially. Every **IoT device, cloud platform, third-party API, and remote worker endpoint** becomes a potential entry point for attackers.

Example: In 2023, a major retailer faced a data breach due to an insecure third-party vendor API, exposing millions of customer records.

2. Sophistication of Cyber Threats

Attackers are no longer lone wolves—they are organized, well-funded, and technologically advanced. Techniques such as **Deepfake AI Manipulation,Advanced Persistent Threats (APTs), AI-generated phishing campaigns, and ransomware-as-a-service (RaaS)** are becoming commonplace.

3. Insider Threats

Not all threats come from external hackers. **Insider threats**, whether malicious or accidental, pose a significant risk to organizations.

An AI Quick Checklist:

- Do employees receive regular cybersecurity training?
- Are access controls implemented effectively?
- Are internal activities monitored for suspicious behavior?

Common Cybersecurity Challenges in Enterprises

1. Balancing Innovation and Security

Organizations often prioritize speed-to-market over cybersecurity, leaving vulnerabilities in new products and platforms.

Example:A fintech startup launched a mobile payment app without adequate security checks, resulting in massive data leaks within weeks of launch.

Strategy Tip: Integrate **security-by-design principles** from day one of any new project.

2. Managing Third-Party Risks

Organizations increasingly rely on third-party vendors for software, data analytics, and infrastructure. Each vendor represents a **potential cybersecurity risk**.

Example:A healthcare provider suffered a breach through a third-party billing software, exposing sensitive patient records.

Best Practice: Implement **Vendor Risk Management (VRM)** processes to assess and monitor third-party cybersecurity hygiene.

3. Lack of Skilled Cybersecurity Talent

Cybersecurity teams are often **overburdened and understaffed**. The global cybersecurity talent gap has left many organizations vulnerable.

The Rise of AI-Driven Cyber Threats

1. AI-Powered Phishing Attacks

Cybercriminals are now using **Generative AI** to create hyper-personalized phishing emails, mimicking the writing style of trusted individuals.

Example: In a recent incident, an AI-generated phishing email bypassed spam filters and tricked employees into sharing sensitive credentials.

Strategy Tip: Train employees to recognize sophisticated phishing attempts and use AI-powered email security tools.

2. Deepfakes and Synthetic Fraud

AI can generate **fake audio, video, or images** to impersonate individuals, creating security breaches.

Example: In 2023, a financial executive was tricked by a deepfake video call into wiring millions to a fraudulent account.

3. Adversarial Attacks on AI Models

Attackers manipulate input data to fool AI models, causing them to make incorrect predictions.

Example: An AI-powered fraud detection model was misled by adversarial inputs, allowing fraudulent transactions to go unnoticed.

How AI is Revolutionizing Cybersecurity

In our increasingly digital-first world, cybersecurity has become a **top priority for enterprises worldwide**. The exponential rise in cyber threats—ranging from ransomware attacks to data breaches—has forced organizations to rethink their security strategies. Enter **Artificial Intelligence (AI)**, a game-changing force that is revolutionizing how businesses defend against cyber threats, protect critical infrastructure, and ensure digital trust.

Traditional cybersecurity approaches relied heavily on **static rule-based systems** and **manual interventions**. While effective in their time, these methods struggle to keep up with today's dynamic threat landscape. AI, with its ability to process vast amounts of data, detect subtle anomalies, and predict potential threats in real-time, offers a **proactive and scalable solution**.

This chapter explores:

- **How AI enhances threat detection, prevention, and response.**
- **The role of AI in adaptive security frameworks.**
- **A Generative AI-powered cybersecurity use case with hands-on Python implementation.**
- **Real-world examples showcasing AI's transformative impact on cybersecurity.**

As we dive in, remember: **Cybersecurity isn't just about technology—it's about resilience, trust, and continuous innovation.**

The Role of AI in Modern Cybersecurity

AI isn't just another cybersecurity tool—it's a **paradigm shift**. Below are key areas where AI is driving significant advancements:

1. Real-Time Threat Detection and Response

AI systems excel at **analyzing massive datasets in real time**, identifying patterns, and flagging anomalies that might go unnoticed by human analysts.

Example: Platforms like **Darktrace** and **IBM Watson for Cybersecurity** use machine learning algorithms to detect potential threats and automatically respond to prevent breaches.

Key Insight:AI-powered threat detection isn't limited to identifying attacks—it predicts and mitigates threats before they escalate.

2. Automating Security Operations Centers (SOCs)

The sheer volume of alerts generated by cybersecurity tools can overwhelm even the best SOC teams. AI automates **threat triaging, log analysis, and alert prioritization**, allowing human analysts to focus on critical incidents.

Example: Cisco's **SecureX** platform leverages AI to reduce false positives and accelerate incident response times.

Quick Fact: Studies show that AI can reduce SOC workload by **up to 80%**.

3. Behavioral Analytics for Insider Threats

Traditional security tools struggle to detect insider threats. AI uses **behavioral analytics** to establish baseline activity patterns and flag deviations.

Example: AI-driven User and Entity Behavior Analytics (UEBA) systems identify suspicious actions, such as unauthorized data access or bulk file downloads.

How well does your current cybersecurity system handle insider threats and behavioral anomalies?

Practical Applications of AI in Cybersecurity

1. Threat Intelligence and Predictive Analytics

AI consolidates data from global threat intelligence feeds, correlating insights and predicting potential attack vectors.

Example: Financial institutions rely on AI systems to predict fraudulent transactions based on historical patterns.

Key Insight: Predictive analytics transforms cybersecurity from a **reactive strategy** into a **proactive shield**.

2. Fraud Detection and Prevention

AI algorithms analyze transactional data in real-time, identifying fraudulent activities with unmatched speed and accuracy.

Example: Mastercard uses AI to analyze billions of transactions daily, preventing unauthorized purchases.

3. Vulnerability Management

AI identifies **vulnerabilities in digital systems** before attackers exploit them. By scanning systems for weak points and recommending patches, AI reduces risk exposure.

Quick Checklist for AI Integration in Cybersecurity:

- Real-time anomaly detection
- Behavioral pattern analysis
- Integration with threat intelligence platforms
- Adaptive threat response mechanisms

Python Implementation: AI-Powered Threat Detection Using Generative AI

Use Case Objective

We'll build a prototype of **Generative AI-powered threat detection system** to:

1. Analyze incoming system logs for anomalies.
2. Classify logs into "Threat" or "Safe."
3. Generate human-readable threat summaries.

Step 1: Import Required Libraries

====================================

```
import pandas as pd
import openai
from sklearn.feature_extraction.text import TfidfVectorizer
from sklearn.metrics.pairwise import cosine_similarity
```

====================================

Step 2: Simulate System Log Data

====================================

```
# Sample log data
data = {
    "log_id": [1, 2, 3],
    "log_text": [
        "Failed login attempt from IP 192.168.1.10",
        "File uploaded to external server",
        "User admin accessed restricted folder"
    ]
}
logs_df = pd.DataFrame(data)
```

====================================

Step 3: Log Classification

```
def classify_log(log_text):
    if "failed login" in log_text.lower() or "external 
server" in log_text.lower():
        return "Threat"
    return "Safe"
logs_df['classification'] = 
logs_df['log_text'].apply(classify_log)
```

====================================

Step 4: Generate Threat Summaries Using Generative AI

====================================

```
openai.api_key = 'your_api_key'
def generate_summary(log_text):
    prompt = f"Explain the security issue: {log_text}"
    response = openai.Completion.create(engine="text-
davinci-003", prompt=prompt, max_tokens=50)
    return response['choices'][0]['text'].strip()
logs_df['summary'] = logs_df.apply(lambda row: 
generate_summary(row['log_text']) if row['classification']
== 'Threat' else "N/A", axis=1)
```

====================================

Step 5: Display Results

====================================

```
print(logs_df[['log_id', 'log_text', 'classification', 
'summary']])
```

====================================

AI is not just an **enhancement to cybersecurity**—it's becoming its **backbone**. By leveraging AI tools, organizations can **predict threats, automate responses, and build trust** in their digital infrastructure.

How can AI-powered cybersecurity solutions improve resilience in your organization?

The Double-Edged Sword of AI Security

Artificial Intelligence (AI) is revolutionizing industries, enhancing decision-making, and optimizing operations. However, **AI systems themselves are vulnerable to unique security risks and adversarial threats**. As organizations increasingly rely on AI for mission-critical operations, ensuring the security, integrity, and reliability of these systems becomes paramount.

Unlike traditional software, AI systems have **dynamic behaviors** influenced by their training data, deployment environments, and real-time inputs. These characteristics introduce **unique vulnerabilities**—from adversarial attacks that manipulate model outputs to data poisoning that corrupts learning mechanisms.

In this chapter, we will:

- Explore the **unique vulnerabilities in AI systems**.
- Examine **common threat vectors** targeting AI models.
- Discuss **best practices for securing AI pipelines, data, and model deployments**.
- Provide **real-world examples and actionable insights** to help leaders safeguard their AI investments.

Understanding Unique Vulnerabilities in AI Systems

Traditional cybersecurity frameworks often fail to address the nuanced vulnerabilities of AI systems. Below are the key areas where AI security diverges from traditional software security:

1. Data Poisoning Attacks

AI models are **only as good as their training data**. If an attacker can inject malicious data into the training pipeline, the resulting model may exhibit **biased, inaccurate, or dangerous behaviors**.

Example:

- In a **spam filter AI**, malicious actors might introduce misleading emails labeled as "safe," causing the model to misclassify future spam.

Mitigation Strategies:

- Regularly validate and audit training datasets.
- Implement **data integrity checks** and anomaly detection mechanisms.

2. Adversarial Attacks

Adversarial attacks involve **crafting malicious inputs** that exploit weaknesses in AI algorithms. A subtle modification to an image or text input can trick an AI model into making incorrect predictions.

Example:

- In **computer vision systems**, adding imperceptible noise to an image can cause an AI to misclassify a stop sign as a yield sign.

Mitigation Strategies:

- Use **adversarial training techniques** to improve model robustness.
- Deploy **input validation mechanisms** to detect manipulated data.

3. Model Inversion Attacks

In this attack, adversaries attempt to **reverse-engineer the AI model's training data** using its outputs. This could lead to the exposure of sensitive or proprietary information.

Example:

- A healthcare AI trained on medical images might inadvertently leak identifiable patient information when queried repeatedly.

Mitigation Strategies:

- Apply **differential privacy techniques** to limit data leakage.
- Implement **rate-limiting and monitoring** on API endpoints.

4. AI Model Theft

Trained AI models are often **valuable intellectual property**. Attackers may attempt to **steal or replicate these models** to gain competitive advantage or cause financial losses.

Example:

- An attacker might reverse-engineer a proprietary AI chatbot model and deploy it elsewhere.

Mitigation Strategies:

- Encrypt AI models at rest and in transit.
- Use **watermarking techniques** to detect unauthorized usage.

How confident are you in the integrity of your AI training and deployment pipelines?

Key Threat Vectors in AI Systems

Understanding how AI systems can be exploited helps organizations build stronger defenses. The primary threat vectors include:

1. Deceptive AI Manipulations

As AI-generated content becomes increasingly sophisticated, bad actors can exploit tools to create **deep fakes**—highly realistic but fabricated media—and **fake brand advertisements**, misleading consumers and tarnishing organizational reputations. These attacks undermine trust and can result in financial losses, regulatory penalties, and damaged brand equity.

Deceptive AI Manipulations

Bad actors exploit advanced AI tools to generate **deep fakes** and **fake brand advertisements**, posing significant risks to businesses and individuals. These manipulations undermine trust, mislead consumers, and can damage reputations or facilitate fraud.

- **Deep Fakes**: AI-generated videos or audio mimicking CEOs or public figures, used to spread disinformation or authorize fraudulent transactions.
- **Fake Brand Ads**: AI-crafted advertisements designed to mimic official branding, often used for phishing, spreading malware, or promoting counterfeit products.

Mitigation

1. AI-Based Detection Tools

- **Deploy deep fake detection systems**: Tools like Microsoft's Video Authenticator or Deeptrace analyze pixel inconsistencies and audio mismatches.
- **Use blockchain for content verification**: Assign digital watermarks to authentic media for verification.

2. Protect Brand Integrity

- **Monitor ad platforms**: Use AI systems to detect unauthorized use of brand assets.
- **Whitelist advertising domains**: Ensure only approved platforms display official ads.

3. Proactive Education

- **Employee training**: Teach teams to recognize manipulations and phishing attempts.
- **Consumer awareness**: Share tips to identify fake ads or media.

By addressing **Deceptive AI Manipulations** through detection, brand protection, and education, businesses can safeguard their operations and maintain trust in an increasingly AI-driven world.

2. Supply Chain Attacks

AI systems often rely on **third-party libraries, pre-trained models, and cloud APIs**. These dependencies can become potential attack surfaces.

Mitigation:

- Regularly audit dependencies and verify third-party components.
- Use trusted repositories and packages.

3. Shadow AI

Employees or teams might deploy AI systems without centralized oversight, leading to **security blind spots**.

Mitigation:

- Establish clear **governance policies** for AI deployments.
- Ensure proper inventory and auditing of all AI projects.

4. Insider Threats

Malicious insiders with access to sensitive AI models and datasets pose significant risks.

Mitigation:

- Implement **role-based access control (RBAC)**.
- Continuously monitor user activities in AI systems.

Quick Checklist for AI Security:

- Is your training data regularly validated?
- Are adversarial training techniques applied?
- Is your AI API secured with authentication and rate-limiting?
- Is there clear governance for AI deployments?

Securing the AI Lifecycle

Securing AI systems isn't limited to a single phase—it spans the **entire AI lifecycle**, from data collection and model training to deployment and ongoing monitoring.

1. Data Security

- Use **encryption for sensitive datasets**.
- Ensure **data provenance tracking** to monitor lineage and changes.

2. Model Security

- Deploy **robust adversarial defenses**.
- Monitor for **model drift and unexpected outputs**.

3. Deployment Security

- Use **secure APIs** with proper authentication and authorization.
- Regularly patch and update models to address vulnerabilities.

4. Monitoring and Auditing

- Implement **continuous monitoring for AI behavior anomalies**.
- Set up **audit trails** to track changes and access patterns.

Building an AI-Driven Cybersecurity Infrastructure

In today's digital-first landscape, the threats are more sophisticated, automated, and AI-powered than ever before. Cybercriminals use generative AI to create deep fakes, phishing emails, and fake brand advertisements, undermining trust and causing financial and reputational damage. To counter this, organizations must adopt an AI-driven cybersecurity infrastructure that is proactive, intelligent, and adaptive. This chapter explores how to design and implement such an infrastructure while addressing modern threats like deep fakes and AI-generated fraud.

Core Components of AI-Driven Cybersecurity Infrastructure

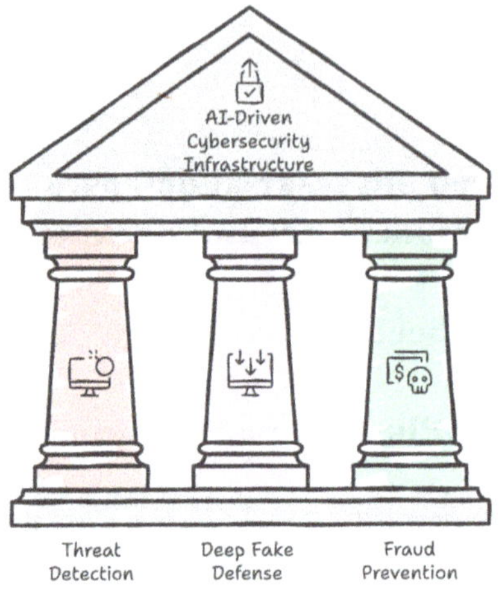

1. **Threat Detection with AI**

AI algorithms excel at identifying patterns and anomalies that might escape traditional rule-based systems. Machine learning models can analyze vast datasets, detect unusual activities, and flag potential threats in real time.

Key Features:

- Behavioral analytics to detect anomalies in user activities.
- AI-powered network intrusion detection systems.
- Real-time threat intelligence from global data sources.

Example: A phishing detection system using NLP to identify fake emails with nuanced linguistic analysis.

2. **Defending Against Deep Fakes and Fake Brand Ads**

Generative AI makes it easy to create convincing deep fakes and counterfeit advertisements that can harm brands and individuals. AI-driven cybersecurity solutions can help detect and mitigate these risks.

High-Level Approach:

- Use AI to detect manipulated media by analyzing inconsistencies in pixelation, audio, and metadata.
- Employ blockchain to verify the authenticity of content and prevent unauthorized changes.
- Monitor ad campaigns for suspicious patterns or unauthorized usage of brand assets.

Real-World Example: Microsoft's Video Authenticator tool that analyzes visual and audio artifacts to detect deep fakes with high accuracy.

3. **AI-Powered Fraud Prevention Systems**

Fraudsters increasingly use AI to bypass traditional defenses. AI-driven fraud detection systems can counter this by analyzing transactions, user behavior, and historical data to identify risks.

Capabilities:

- Predictive models for identifying transaction anomalies.
- Multi-factor authentication enhanced with AI-powered biometric verification.
- AI-based risk scoring for customer accounts.

Example: PayPal's AI-driven fraud detection system, which evaluates billions of transactions to prevent fraud in real time.

Designing an AI-Driven Cybersecurity Infrastructure

The infrastructure for AI-driven cybersecurity integrates various components to create a multi-layered defense mechanism.

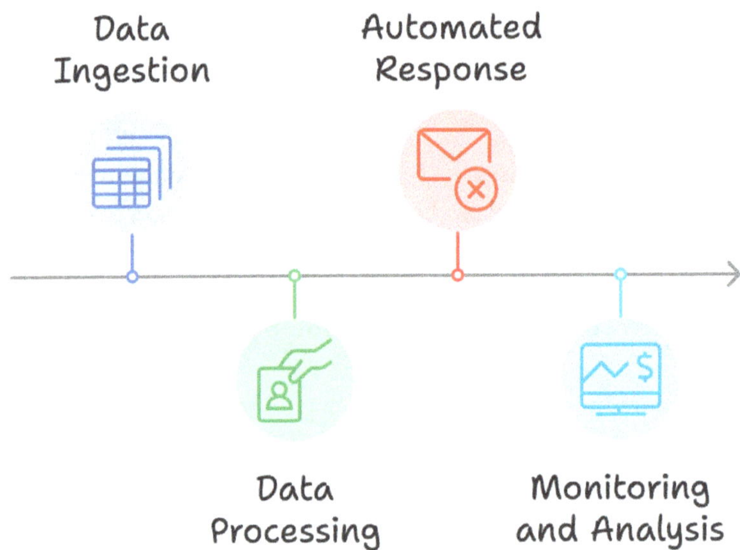

Key Elements:

1. **Data Ingestion Layer**: Aggregates data from endpoints, networks, and third-party threat intelligence feeds.
2. **AI Analytics Engine**: Processes the data for threat detection, anomaly analysis, and pattern recognition.
3. **Automation Layer**: Automates response workflows such as isolating infected systems or blocking malicious IPs.
4. **Visualization and Reporting**: Provides dashboards for real-time monitoring and decision-making.

High-Level Workflow:

1. Threat intelligence feeds and raw data enter the **Data Ingestion Layer**.
2. Machine learning models in the **AI Analytics Engine** process the data, flagging anomalies and identifying threats.
3. Identified threats trigger automated actions through the **Automation Layer**, such as alerting teams or blocking access.
4. **Visualization and Reporting**enables decision-makers to view real-time updates and analyze historical data for trends.

Implementation Challenges and Mitigation Strategies

Challenge 1: Data Overload

AI models require large datasets for training and operation, but unstructured or irrelevant data can overwhelm systems.

Solution:

- Employ pre-processing pipelines to clean and standardize data.
- Use data prioritization algorithms to focus on high-risk sources.

Challenge 2: Model Bias and False Positives

AI models may generate false positives or fail to generalize across diverse scenarios.

Solution:

- Regularly retrain models with diverse datasets.
- Implement human-in-the-loop (HITL) systems for critical decision-making.

Challenge 3: Sophisticated AI-Powered Attacks

Cybercriminals are leveraging generative AI to bypass defenses and launch unprecedented attacks.

Solution:

- Employ adversarial training to expose AI models to potential attack patterns.
- Invest in offensive AI tools that predict and simulate cyber threats before they occur.

In light of existing threats, leader should reflect on following question:

1. **Proactive vs Reactive**: Is your current cybersecurity strategy focused on detecting threats after they occur or preventing them proactively?
2. **Deep Fake Resilience**: How robust are your systems against AI-generated media threats?
3. **AI and Automation**: Are you using AI not just to detect but also to respond to threats in real time?

The Future of AI-Driven Cybersecurity

Building an AI-driven cybersecurity infrastructure is no longer optional—it is a necessity. As cyber threats become smarter, organizations must leverage AI to stay ahead. From deep fakes to fraudulent ads, AI provides the tools to detect and defend against modern threats. By integrating AI at every layer of cybersecurity, businesses can safeguard their assets, protect their reputation, and ensure a resilient digital future.

With the right vision, strategy, and execution, AI can transform cybersecurity from a reactive function into a proactive, intelligent defense mechanism that inspires confidence and trust in the digital age.

ROI of AI-Powered Cybersecurity

AI-powered cybersecurity has transformed from a mere cost center into a value-driven asset. With the advent of generative AI (Gen AI), organizations can leverage next-gen tools for real-time threat detection, proactive defense, and optimized operations. However, as capabilities expand, so do associated costs and complexities. This chapter explores the evolving cost-benefit paradigm, emphasizing how Gen AI reshapes ROI measurement in cybersecurity.

How AI Impacts Cybersecurity ROI

Generative AI introduces advanced capabilities, fundamentally altering how cybersecurity teams measure return on investment (ROI). Unlike traditional AI and ML systems that are primarily reactive, Gen AI enables proactive and adaptive strategies, such as generating human-readable threat insights and orchestrating dynamic response mechanisms. Here's how this transition impacts ROI:

1. **Proactive Threat Management**
   - Gen AI reduces attack surfaces by identifying vulnerabilities and potential threats before they materialize. For instance, it can simulate phishing emails and deepfake attacks, helping organizations fortify their defenses preemptively. This minimizes damage and operational disruptions.
2. **Enhanced Analyst Productivity**
   - Gen AI reduces repetitive tasks, such as log analysis, by providing dynamic summaries and actionable insights. Teams can allocate resources more strategically, focusing on high-value activities rather than manual triage.
3. **Improved Detection Accuracy**
   - By using multimodal inputs (text, images, and behavior patterns), Gen AI systems reduce false positives, saving costs associated with wasted investigation time. Higher accuracy results in fewer breaches, contributing to measurable savings.
4. **Customer Confidence and Compliance**
   - Gen AI-generated explainable insights build trust among customers and regulators, ensuring organizations maintain their reputations while avoiding costly fines for non-compliance.

8

The Future of Generative AI – Emerging Trends and Opportunities

"We must prepare for a future where the only constant is intelligent systems continuously reshaping our world."

Demis Hassabis

Generative AI has moved past its experimental phase and firmly established itself as a transformative force across industries. From text-to-image models that challenge creative boundaries to AI agents autonomously performing complex workflows, the landscape is evolving faster than most organizations can keep up.

But what lies ahead? Will generative AI remain confined to chatbots and creative tools, or will it evolve into **autonomous agents managing entire supply chains or predicting financial crashes before they happen**?

This chapter explores **emerging trends**, **groundbreaking use cases**, and **potential disruptions**, offering tech leaders and strategists a **roadmap to prepare for the future of AI innovation**.

Trend 1: New Cost Metrics to Factor in with AI

Adopting Generative AI introduces several cost considerations beyond traditional AI systems:

1. **LLM Training and Hosting**
    - **Training Costs**: Training large models like GPT demands immense GPU power and energy, often costing millions.
    - **Hosting Costs**: Deploying models in real-time requires robust cloud infrastructure, leading to ongoing expenses.
2. **Token-Based Pricing**
    - **Inference Costs**: Many providers charge per token, and high-traffic use cases like chatbots can drive costs up.
    - **Optimization**: Techniques like caching and prompt engineering can mitigate token expenses but require upfront investments.
3. **Fine-Tuning and Customization**
    - Adapting models to specific needs requires skilled talent, domain-specific data, and periodic updates.
4. **Data Preparation**
    - High-quality training datasets, often involving annotation or synthetic data, incur significant costs.
5. **Compliance and Security**
    - Ensuring legal compliance (e.g., GDPR) and securing AI systems against attacks adds operational complexity.
6. **Operational Maintenance**
    - Regular updates, bug fixes, and integration into enterprise systems lead to recurring expenses.
7. **Talent and Training**
    - Hiring AI experts and training employees on Gen AI systems adds both upfront and ongoing costs.

Key Considerations

1. Leverage open-source models to minimize licensing fees.
2. Prioritize ROI assessment early to align costs with potential benefits.
3. Plan for long-term operational and scaling expenses.

By understanding and addressing these costs, organizations can maximize the value of their Gen AI investments while maintaining financial sustainability.

Trend 2: Autonomous AI Agents – The Rise of Digital Co-Workers

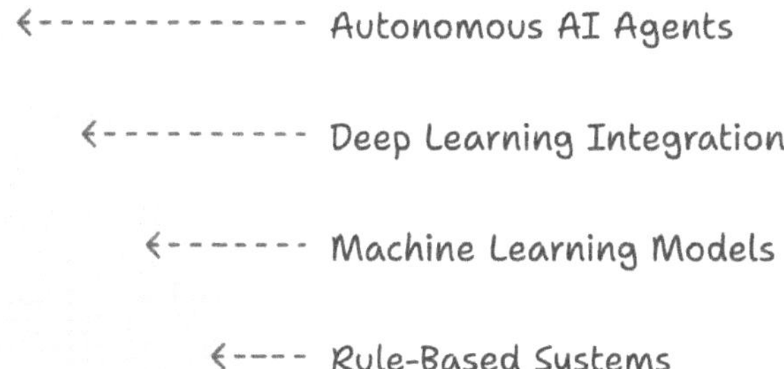

The Dawn of Autonomous AI Agents

Imagine a world where AI agents act as reliable digital co-workers — automating complex tasks, making data-driven decisions, and collaborating seamlessly with human teams. This vision is no longer confined to science fiction; it's unfolding in front of us. From **AutoGPT** to **BabyAGI**, AI agents are transitioning from theoretical models to **real-world problem solvers** across industries.

These agents are not just glorified chatbots; they are **task-oriented systems capable of planning, reasoning, and executing multi-step workflows autonomously**. Whether it's handling customer service tickets, managing cloud deployments, or optimizing supply chains in real-time, **AI agents are revolutionizing how work gets done.**

This chapter delves into the rise of autonomous AI agents, their capabilities, practical applications, and how organizations can prepare to integrate them effectively.

Understanding Autonomous AI Agents

At their core, autonomous AI agents are **self-operating AI systems** equipped with the ability to:

1. **Perceive** their environment (e.g., reading emails, monitoring dashboards).
2. **Plan** a series of tasks to achieve a goal.
3. **Act** to execute tasks without human intervention.
4. **Learn** from feedback and improve over time.

These agents operate on a combination of **large language models (LLMs)**, **retrieval-augmented generation (RAG)**, and **reinforcement learning from human feedback (RLHF)** to maximize their efficiency and adaptability.

Key Features of AI Agents:

- **Autonomy:**Operate without constant human supervision.
- **Adaptability:**Adjust their workflow based on new data or task changes.
- **Goal-Oriented Behavior:**Complete specific objectives set by users or organizational workflows.
- **Scalability:**Perform repetitive or large-scale tasks efficiently.

Real-World Applications of Autonomous AI Agents

1. Customer Support Automation

Imagine an AI agent managing customer inquiries, escalating only critical issues to human agents. For example, **Salesforce Einstein Bots** use AI agents to resolve 80% of common queries without human intervention.

2. IT Operations Management

In cloud deployments, **AI Ops agents** can monitor system health, detect anomalies, and automatically initiate corrective actions. Platforms like **Dynatrace AI** are leading this space.

3. Autonomous Financial Advisory

Investment platforms are now deploying AI agents to provide **portfolio recommendations, monitor stock performance, and send risk alerts** — all in real time.

4. Supply Chain Optimization

Autonomous agents are analyzing real-time inventory data, predicting disruptions, and optimizing procurement. For example, **Blue Yonder AI agents** help optimize logistics workflows at scale.

Preparing Your Organization for Autonomous AI Agents

Step 1: Define Clear Use Cases

Start with specific, well-scoped tasks that can be handed over to AI agents. For example:

- Automating repetitive back-office workflows.
- Real-time analysis of sales data for inventory optimization.

Step 2: Build a Tech-Ready Infrastructure

- Adopt **API-first architectures** to enable seamless integration with AI agents.
- Invest in **cloud computing capabilities** for large-scale deployments.
- Utilize **vector databases** to store agent insights efficiently.

Step 3: Upskill Teams for AI Agent Integration
Ensure teams understand:

- How AI agents work.
- How to set tasks and interpret AI outputs.
- Ethical and compliance considerations.

Step 4: Implement Monitoring and Guardrails

- Continuous evaluation of agent outputs.
- Ethical oversight for unintended consequences.
- Real-time intervention frameworks.

Case Study: Autonomous Agents in Financial Risk Management

Scenario:

A leading financial institution deployed an **AI risk management agent** to monitor global stock markets and predict asset volatility.

Before AI Agents:

- Analysts manually monitored dashboards.
- Decisions were delayed during market volatility.

After Deploying AI Agents:

- Real-time monitoring of global financial indicators.
- Instant alerts on high-risk transactions.
- Autonomous rebalancing of portfolios to mitigate risks.

Results:

- 40% reduction in response time during market anomalies.
- 25% increase in accuracy of asset risk predictions.

Challenges and Limitations of Autonomous AI Agents

While autonomous AI agents hold immense promise, they also come with **unique challenges:**

1. **Lack of Contextual Understanding:** AI agents may misinterpret ambiguous scenarios.
2. **Ethical Boundaries:** Without proper oversight, agents might make decisions misaligned with organizational values.
3. **Integration Complexity:** Legacy systems may pose challenges for seamless AI agent integration.
4. **Security Risks:** Agents interacting across systems are vulnerable to cyber-attacks.

Checklist: Key Questions Before Deploying AI Agents

- Are the tasks clearly defined and well-scoped?
- Are ethical guardrails in place for autonomous decision-making?

The Future of Autonomous AI Agents

The future of AI agents lies in **collaborative intelligence** — where AI agents and humans work side by side, amplifying each other's strengths.

Upcoming Trends in AI Agents:

1. **Cross-Platform Integration:**Agents managing workflows across multiple business systems.
2. **Advanced Reasoning Capabilities:**Multi-step problem-solving with minimal guidance.
3. **Emotionally Intelligent Agents:**Understanding human emotions and adapting responses in customer-facing tasks.

Embracing Autonomous AI Agents

Autonomous AI agents are not replacements for human workers — they are **enhancements, enablers, and collaborators**. They promise:

- **Higher Operational Efficiency:**Handling routine tasks at scale.
- **Faster Decision-Making:**Real-time analysis and response.
- **Scalable Workflows:**Handling tasks beyond human capacity.

Key Action Steps:

1. Identify tasks suitable for AI agent automation.
2. Ensure the infrastructure supports large-scale AI workflows.
3. Build governance and monitoring layers for AI agent activity.
4. Continuously iterate and refine AI agent goals and outputs.

The era of autonomous AI agents is here. Organizations that harness their potential today will define the benchmarks of tomorrow.

Trend 3: Multimodal AI – Beyond Text and Images

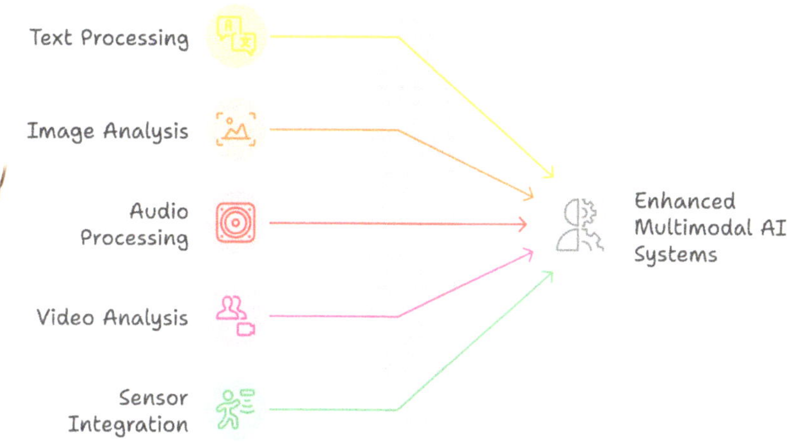

In an era where **information flows across text, images, videos, sounds, and even sensor data**, relying on single-mode AI systems is no longer sufficient. Enter **Multimodal AI** — systems capable of processing and understanding information from multiple types of data sources simultaneously.

Imagine an AI model that can:

- **Read a medical report**(text), **analyze an MRI scan** (image), and **detect anomalies from audio recordings** (sound).
- **Watch a customer service video call**, **analyze voice tones**, and **respond with context-aware suggestions**.

Multimodal AI transcends traditional AI boundaries, enabling richer, more nuanced understanding and problem-solving capabilities. With advancements in models like **OpenAI's GPT-4**,

Google's Gemini, and **DeepMind's Flamingo**, multimodal AI is fast becoming the standard for real-world AI applications.

This chapter explores the rise of multimodal AI, its technical foundations, real-world applications, and actionable strategies for integrating it into enterprise workflows.

What is Multimodal AI?

At its core, **Multimodal AI** refers to AI systems that can **understand, interpret, and generate data across multiple modalities** — such as text, images, videos, speech, and sensor signals — to perform tasks more effectively.

Key Modalities in Multimodal AI:

1. **Text:**Language models for analysis, summarization, and dialogue.
2. **Images:**Object recognition, scene understanding, and image generation.
3. **Audio:**Voice recognition, emotion detection, and sound analysis.
4. **Video:**Action recognition, object tracking, and contextual understanding.
5. **Sensor Data:**IoT readings, biometric data, and environmental signals.

How It Works:

Multimodal models fuse information from different modalities into a **shared representation space**. This allows them to:

- Contextually understand relationships between different data types.
- Generate coherent and contextually aware outputs.
- Adapt to diverse use cases seamlessly.

Example: A multimodal AI system analyzing a live sports event might:

- Understand commentary (text/audio).
- Track player movements (video).
- Recognize player emotions via facial analysis (image).

Real-World Applications of Multimodal AI

1. Healthcare Diagnostics

Scenario:A multimodal AI system analyzes a patient's health history (text), CT scans (image), and heart sounds (audio) to deliver a holistic diagnosis.

Impact: Improved diagnostic accuracy and early detection of diseases.

2. E-Commerce Search and Recommendations

Scenario:A user uploads a picture of a dress, describes the color and style preferences, and expects matching product suggestions.

Impact: Enhanced user experience and increased sales conversions.

3. Autonomous Vehicles

Scenario: Multimodal AI combines visual data from cameras, LiDAR readings, and GPS signals to navigate traffic safely.

Impact: Safer self-driving capabilities.

4. Smart Customer Support Agents

Scenario: During a video call, a multimodal AI agent detects frustration in the user's voice, cross-references their purchase history (text), and suggests solutions in real-time.

Impact: Improved customer satisfaction.

How could multimodal AI improve existing customer service or diagnostic workflows in your organization?

Building Multimodal AI Systems in Enterprises

Adopting multimodal AI involves significant technical, organizational, and infrastructural considerations. Below are key building blocks:

1. Data Integration Across Modalities

- Centralize data from text, images, audio, and sensor inputs into unified data lakes.
- Ensure data quality, consistency, and interoperability across different sources.

2. Infrastructure for Processing and Storage

- Use **high-performance GPUs** for parallel processing of multimodal data.
- Implement **vector databases** for efficient embedding storage and retrieval.

3. Pre-Trained Multimodal Models

- Leverage pre-trained models like **CLIP**, **DALL-E**, or **Google Gemini**.
- Fine-tune these models on domain-specific datasets for better performance.

4. Cross-Functional Collaboration

- Build cross-functional teams combining data scientists, designers, and domain experts.
- Ensure alignment on business objectives for multimodal AI projects.

Checklist for Adopting Multimodal AI:

- Are multimodal datasets readily accessible?
- Is your infrastructure capable of handling high-dimensional data processing?
- Do you have the expertise to fine-tune multimodal AI models?

Case Study: Multimodal AI in Retail

Scenario: Enhancing In-Store Experience with Multimodal AI

A global retail chain deployed a multimodal AI system to improve in-store experiences:

1. **Text Data:**Analyzing customer reviews and survey responses.
2. **Image Data:**Identifying product stock levels via shelf cameras.
3. **Audio Data:**Detecting audio cues from customer conversations with staff.
4. **Sensor Data:**Monitoring store foot traffic using IoT devices.

Results:

- Real-time insights into customer preferences.
- Proactive inventory restocking.
- Enhanced in-store customer engagement strategies.

Challenges in Multimodal AI Adoption

While the promise of multimodal AI is immense, organizations face key hurdles:

1. **Data Silos:**Fragmented storage systems hinder unified data processing.

2. **Computational Costs:**Training multimodal models is resource-intensive.
3. **Interpretability Issues:**Decoding how AI arrives at multimodal insights can be challenging.
4. **Data Privacy:**Combining data from multiple sources raises security concerns.

Quick Mitigation Strategies:

- Invest in unified data architectures.
- Optimize pre-trained models instead of training from scratch.
- Implement robust AI governance frameworks for transparency and oversight.

What key challenges might arise in deploying multimodal AI in your current tech stack?

The Future of Multimodal AI

The evolution of multimodal AI points toward a **seamless integration of human-like perception and machine intelligence.**

Emerging Trends:

1. **Real-Time Multimodal Interaction:**AI responding to real-time events across multiple channels simultaneously.
2. **Emotionally Aware AI:**Understanding emotional cues from facial expressions and voice tones.
3. **Digital Twins Enhanced by Multimodality:**Virtual replicas of systems enhanced with multimodal AI for predictive insights.

Preparing for the Multimodal Future:

- Foster data-driven cultures ready for multimodal systems.
- Align technical infrastructure for scalability.
- Encourage interdisciplinary innovation.

Multimodal AI represents a **fundamental leap in AI capabilities**, enabling businesses to:

- Gain deeper insights across diverse data sources.
- Improve customer experience with context-aware systems.
- Make faster, data-driven decisions at scale.

The time to adopt multimodal AI is now. Leaders who invest in multimodal technologies today will have a significant edge tomorrow.

Trend 4: Real-Time AI – Instant Adaptation and Insights

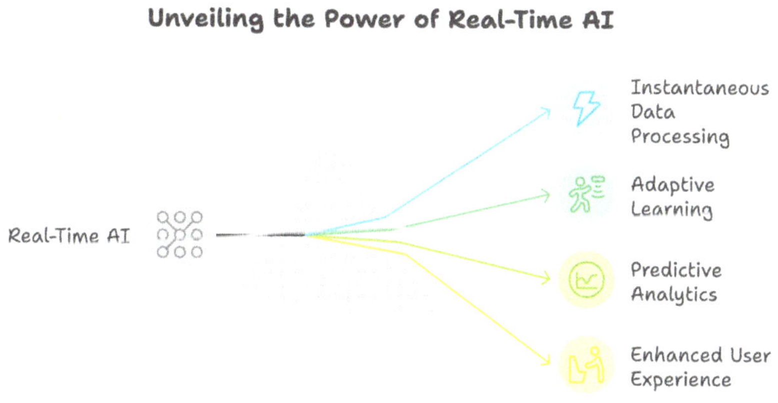

Unveiling the Power of Real-Time AI

Real-Time AI
Instantaneous Data Processing
Adaptive Learning
Predictive Analytics
Enhanced User Experience

In a world where **every second counts**, delayed decisions can mean missed opportunities, increased costs, or even catastrophic failures. Enter **Real-Time AI** — systems capable of **processing, analyzing, and responding to data in milliseconds**.

Imagine:

- A **financial trading platform** adjusting investment strategies based on live market data.
- A **retail website** dynamically repricing products based on competitor pricing and customer behavior.
- A **self-driving car** instantly responding to sudden obstacles on the road.

Real-Time AI is transforming industries by delivering **immediate insights** and enabling **instant decision-making**. This chapter explores the core capabilities of Real-Time AI, practical applications, technical underpinnings, and the strategic importance of adopting real-time systems in enterprise workflows.

What is Real-Time AI?

Real-Time AI refers to AI systems designed to **ingest, process, and respond to data streams with minimal latency**. Unlike traditional AI models that operate in batch mode or periodic intervals, Real-Time AI offers **immediacy and adaptability**.

Core Characteristics of Real-Time AI:

1. **Low Latency:** Decisions are made in milliseconds.
2. **Continuous Learning:** Models adapt to new data in real-time.
3. **Dynamic Decision-Making:** Instant adaptation to changing environments.
4. **Scalable Infrastructure:** Supports high-volume, high-velocity data streams.

How it Works:

- **Data Streaming:** Real-time data ingestion from IoT sensors, databases, and APIs.
- **Edge Processing:** Running AI algorithms closer to the data source for reduced latency.
- **Instant Feedback Loops:** Continuous performance monitoring and optimization.

Example: A fraud detection system in a banking app detects suspicious activity (e.g., sudden overseas transactions) and blocks the card immediately, preventing unauthorized access.

Real-World Applications of Real-Time AI

1. Financial Trading Platforms

Scenario: AI algorithms analyze live stock market data, predict price movements, and execute trades within milliseconds.

Impact: Optimized trading strategies and reduced financial risk.

2. Smart Manufacturing (Industry 4.0)

Scenario: IoT devices feed real-time machine data into AI systems that predict equipment failure before it happens.

Impact: Minimized downtime and increased productivity.

3. E-Commerce Dynamic Pricing

Scenario: AI monitors competitor prices, adjusts product pricing dynamically, and tailors offers based on user behavior.

Impact: Increased sales and optimized profit margins.

4. Real-Time Fraud Detection in Banking

Scenario: AI flags unusual patterns in live transaction data and prevents fraudulent activities immediately.

Impact: Enhanced security and reduced financial losses.

5. Healthcare Monitoring

Scenario: Wearable devices send real-time health data to AI systems that alert doctors about irregularities (e.g., abnormal heart rates).

Impact: Faster medical interventions and improved patient outcomes.

Technical Foundations of Real-Time AI

Building Real-Time AI systems requires a combination of **advanced infrastructure, robust algorithms, and seamless integration with data streams**.

1. Data Streaming Pipelines

- **Tools:**Apache Kafka, Amazon Kinesis, Google Cloud Pub/Sub
- **Purpose:**Enable continuous data ingestion and processing.

2. Edge AI Processing

- **Concept:**AI algorithms deployed closer to the data source (e.g., IoT edge devices).
- **Benefits:**Reduces latency and network dependency.

3. Real-Time Model Serving

- **Tools:**TensorFlow Serving, TorchServe, ONNX Runtime
- **Purpose:**Serve AI models in real-time with optimized latency.

4. Dynamic Feedback Loops

- **Concept:**Continuous performance evaluation and retraining based on live data.

- **Benefits:**Models adapt to changing patterns in real time.

Checklist for Real-Time AI Adoption:

- Is your data infrastructure capable of real-time ingestion and processing?
- Do you have edge computing capabilities where latency is critical?
- Are your AI models optimized for real-time serving and decision-making?

Case Study: Real-Time AI in Retail for Personalized Recommendations

Scenario: Personalized Shopping Experiences in Real-Time

A global e-commerce giant implemented Real-Time AI for personalized product recommendations:

1. **Data Sources:**Live user browsing behavior, purchase history, and cart activity.
2. **Real-Time Processing:**Algorithms dynamically generate recommendations based on user clicks and scrolling behavior.
3. **Instant Feedback Loop:**Recommendations are refined in real-time based on user actions.

Results:

- **30% increase in conversion rates.**
- **Enhanced customer satisfaction due to hyper-relevant suggestions.**

Challenges in Real-Time AI Adoption

While Real-Time AI offers transformative capabilities, organizations often encounter the following challenges:

1. **Infrastructure Complexity:**
   - Real-time systems require high-performance infrastructure and robust data streaming pipelines.
2. **High Computational Costs:**
   - Real-time processing consumes significant computational resources.
3. **Data Governance and Compliance:**
   - Continuous data ingestion raises privacy and security concerns.
4. **Model Drift:**
   - Models can become less effective if not continuously retrained.

Quick Mitigation Strategies:

- Leverage **cloud-based real-time infrastructure** (e.g., AWS, Azure).
- Use **optimized AI serving tools** (e.g., ONNX Runtime).
- Implement **privacy-first architectures** to address compliance concerns.

The Future of Real-Time AI

The next frontier of Real-Time AI will blur the lines between **human intuition and machine intelligence**.

Emerging Trends:

1. **Hyper-Personalization:** Real-time AI will deliver experiences uniquely tailored to individuals at scale.
2. **AI-Powered Decision Intelligence:** Instant insights will drive executive decision-making.

3. **Edge-AI Proliferation:** Smart edge devices will dominate real-time AI deployment.

Preparing for the Real-Time AI Revolution:

- Build **scalable real-time data architectures**.
- Invest in **AI-ready infrastructure**.
- Foster a **culture of real-time agility** in decision-making processes.

Real-Time AI is not just an incremental upgrade — it's a **paradigm shift** in how businesses make decisions, respond to challenges, and seize opportunities.

Key Takeaways:

- **Real-time AI enables instant, data-driven decision-making.**
- **Adopting real-time AI requires robust infrastructure and agile workflows.**
- **Future-ready organizations must prioritize real-time responsiveness in their AI strategy.**

Embrace the power of **Real-Time AI** today, and your organization will be equipped to lead in an ever-accelerating digital world.

Trend 5: Ethical AI and Governance – Building Public Trust

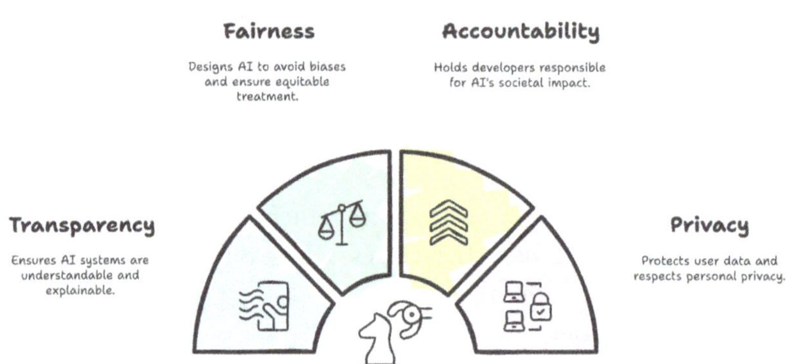

In a world where artificial intelligence increasingly influences our daily lives—from personalized healthcare recommendations to financial loan approvals—**trust has become the currency of successful AI adoption.** As organizations rush to implement AI solutions, the need for **ethical AI practices** and robust **governance frameworks** has never been more critical.

Why Ethical AI Matters:

- AI systems often make decisions that directly impact people's lives.
- Ethical lapses can lead to reputational damage, financial losses, and regulatory backlash.
- Without transparency, users may reject AI systems, limiting their adoption and impact.

Real-World Snapshot:

In 2023, an AI recruitment tool was discovered to have gender bias, favoring male candidates for technical roles. The scandal forced the organization to shut down the tool, issue public apologies, and face regulatory scrutiny.

Key Lesson: Ethical lapses in AI aren't just technical flaws—they're cultural and organizational failures.

In this chapter, we'll explore how ethical AI principles and governance frameworks can guide organizations to build trustworthy AI systems that align with societal values and regulatory expectations.

What is Ethical AI?

Ethical AI refers to designing, developing, and deploying AI systems in ways that prioritize:

- **Fairness:** Eliminating biases and ensuring equal treatment across demographics.
- **Transparency:** Making AI decision-making processes clear and understandable.
- **Accountability:** Assigning responsibility for AI outcomes.
- **Privacy:** Respecting and safeguarding user data.

The Pillars of Ethical AI:

1. **Fairness and Bias Mitigation:** AI systems must not discriminate based on gender, race, age, or socioeconomic status.
2. **Transparency:** Clear documentation and communication about how AI decisions are made.
3. **Privacy and Data Protection:** Compliance with regulations like **GDPR** and **CCPA** to ensure user privacy.

4. **Accountability:** Clear governance on who takes responsibility when AI fails.

Does your organization have an ethical AI charter or policy in place?

Why AI Governance Matters

AI governance ensures that AI systems operate within ethical, legal, and business boundaries. It's about setting **rules, roles, and responsibilities** to manage AI's risks and rewards effectively.

Key Goals of AI Governance:

1. **Risk Management:**Proactively identifying and mitigating AI risks.
2. **Compliance:**Adhering to global AI regulations and standards.
3. **Operational Oversight:**Monitoring AI systems in production to detect anomalies.
4. **Alignment with Business Goals:**Ensuring AI initiatives align with strategic objectives.

Case Example: IBM's AI Ethics Board

IBM established an **AI Ethics Board** to oversee the responsible development of AI products. The board conducts regular audits, sets guidelines, and ensures ethical risks are proactively managed.

Quick Checklist:

- Does your organization have an AI governance policy?
- Are stakeholders from diverse teams (tech, legal, HR, compliance) involved in governance?
- Are AI models reviewed periodically for compliance and fairness?

Implementing Ethical AI in Organizations

1. Build Cross-Functional AI Ethics Committees

Include stakeholders from engineering, legal, compliance, and HR to collectively evaluate AI risks and ethical concerns.

2. Develop Ethical AI Frameworks

- Follow established frameworks like **EU's AI Act**, **NIST AI Risk Management Framework**, or **ISO/IEC 42001**.
- Create internal guidelines tailored to your business context.

3. Audit and Monitor Regularly

Conduct routine ethical AI audits to ensure compliance with frameworks and address unintended consequences.

4. Educate and Train Teams

Train technical and non-technical teams on AI ethics to embed awareness at all organizational levels.

Who is responsible for ethical oversight in your AI projects?

Building Public Trust Through Transparency

The Transparency Imperative

- Users must understand how AI systems arrive at decisions.
- Transparency builds credibility, reduces fear, and fosters adoption.

Strategies for Transparency:

1. **Explainable AI (XAI):** Use tools like **SHAP (SHapley Additive exPlanations)** and **LIME (Local Interpretable Model-Agnostic Explanations)** to make AI decisions understandable.
2. **Open Communication:** Clearly explain the scope, capabilities, and limitations of AI systems to customers and stakeholders.
3. **Public AI Reports:** Publish regular transparency reports about AI performance, biases detected, and steps taken to address them.

Case Study: Google's Explainable AI Framework

Google's Explainable AI tools allow organizations to understand and interpret model predictions, increasing transparency across AI systems.

Quick Tip:

Include transparency as a KPI when measuring AI project success.

Regulations Shaping Ethical AI
Global Regulatory Landscape:

1. **European Union AI Act:** A risk-based regulation categorizing AI systems into unacceptable, high-risk, and low-risk categories.
2. **GDPR (General Data Protection Regulation):** Emphasizes user consent and data privacy.
3. **California Consumer Privacy Act (CCPA):** Grants consumers greater control over personal data.
4. **Singapore Model AI Governance Framework:** Encourages companies to align AI with ethical principles.

Practical Steps for Compliance:

- Regular AI audits for fairness and bias.
- Transparency documentation for every AI model.
- Clear user consent protocols.

Overcoming Challenges in Ethical AI Adoption
Common Challenges:

1. **Bias in Data and Algorithms:** Legacy biases in training data.
2. **Lack of Accountability:** Undefined ownership for AI outcomes.
3. **Limited Awareness:** Teams unaware of AI's ethical risks.
4. **Regulatory Uncertainty:** Constantly evolving legal requirements.

Solutions:

- Invest in high-quality, diverse datasets.
- Designate an **AI Ethics Officer** or similar role.
- Build AI literacy among business stakeholders.

The Business Case for Ethical AI

Ethical AI isn't just a compliance requirement—it's a **competitive advantage**.

Key Benefits:

- **Enhanced Brand Reputation:** Ethical AI builds public trust.
- **Reduced Legal and Compliance Risks:** Minimize penalties and legal scrutiny.
- **Higher Adoption Rates:** Users trust transparent systems.
- **Sustainable AI Deployment:** Ethical frameworks create long-lasting AI systems.

Real-World Insight:

Microsoft has integrated ethical AI principles across all products, enhancing user trust and reducing backlash in sensitive applications like facial recognition technology.

Key Learnings from the Chapter:

- Ethical AI and robust governance frameworks are essential for long-term AI success.
- Transparency and accountability foster trust among users and stakeholders.
- Regulatory compliance ensures responsible deployment of AI solutions.

Start building your **AI Ethics and Governance Playbook** today. Ethical AI isn't just a checkbox—it's the foundation for sustainable innovation.

9

Final Thoughts – Leading the AI Revolution

"Change is the law of life. And those who look only to the past or present are certain to miss the future."

John F. Kennedy

As we reach the final chapter of the book, it's time to pause, reflect, and synthesize the core insights from our journey together. Whether you're a **tech leader orchestrating AI transformation**, a **business executive shaping AI strategies**, or a **data scientist building innovative AI solutions**, this chapter serves as a guidepost—a moment to distill the lessons learned and prepare for the path ahead.

The horizon of AI isn't static; it's constantly evolving, shaped by **technological innovation**, **ethical considerations**, and **human ingenuity**.

Key Lessons from the AI Journey

Throughout this book, we've covered the foundational pillars, strategic insights, and actionable use cases for adopting and scaling AI effectively. Here are the **core lessons** you should carry forward:

1. AI is Not Just Technology—It's a Cultural Shift

AI adoption begins with a **cultural mindset**. Organizations that foster a **culture of curiosity, experimentation, and collaboration** are the ones that succeed in scaling AI across their value chain.

Does your organization view AI as just a tool, or as a fundamental driver of cultural transformation?

2. Governance and Ethics Are Non-Negotiable

AI governance isn't a checkbox—it's an ongoing commitment to **fairness, accountability, transparency, and compliance**. Ethical AI isn't just about preventing harm; it's about actively doing good.

Quick Tip:

Build AI governance teams and prioritize transparency tools to explain AI decisions clearly to stakeholders.

3. Scalability is the North Star

Pilot projects are great for experimentation, but the true value of AI emerges when solutions can scale across departments, geographies, and customer segments.

Key Action Point:

Ensure every AI pilot has a **scaling roadmap** and **defined KPIs** to measure long-term success.

11.2 Building AI Resilience: Preparing for Uncertainty

In the face of **technological uncertainty, regulatory changes, and evolving threats**, resilience is key.

Key Strategies for AI Resilience:

- **Diversify AI Tools & Models:**Avoid dependence on a single vendor or platform.
- **Focus on Data Integrity:**Build systems to continuously clean, validate, and enrich data.
- **Implement Real-Time Monitoring:**Proactively identify AI drift, anomalies, and biases.

Future-Proofing Your AI Strategy

1. Stay Agile and Adaptive

Adopting AI isn't a one-time event—it's a continuous cycle of **iteration, optimization, and scaling**. Keep refining your AI strategy as new trends and tools emerge.

2. Talent is the Competitive Edge

Invest in AI talent pipelines, upskilling programs, and cross-functional AI fluency.

3. Ethical AI Should Be Embedded, Not Bolted On

Ethics should be a core principle, not an afterthought. Build systems that prioritize responsible AI practices from day one.

Quick Tip:

Start every AI project with an ethical review process to identify potential risks and mitigations.

Measuring Success: The Right Metrics Matter

AI Metrics That Drive Real Business Impact:

- **ROI on AI Initiatives:** Are your AI projects generating measurable business value?
- **Adoption Rate:** Are teams actively using AI tools in their workflows?

- **User Satisfaction:** Are customers or internal stakeholders benefiting from AI outcomes?
- **Model Accuracy & Fairness:** Are AI predictions reliable, unbiased, and explainable?

Quick Tip:
Create **AI Performance Dashboards** to provide transparency on these metrics to all stakeholders.

Balancing Innovation and Responsibility

Innovation drives AI forward, but responsibility ensures it's sustainable. Organizations must balance:

- **Speed vs. Caution:** Innovate boldly but test rigorously.
- **Profit vs. Purpose:** Drive revenue without compromising on ethics.
- **Automation vs. Human Touch:** Leverage AI for efficiency while preserving human creativity and empathy.

Does your AI strategy strike the right balance between innovation and responsibility?

The Human Factor in an AI World

AI isn't about replacing humans—it's about **augmenting human potential**. Leaders, employees, and stakeholders must:

- Embrace AI as a collaborative partner, not a competitor.
- Foster transparency and trust in AI systems.
- Build emotional intelligence alongside AI intelligence.

Key Insight:

The most successful AI transformations aren't technology-first; they're **people-first**.

Global AI Collaboration: Shaping the Future Together

The future of AI will depend on collaboration across:

- **Governments and Regulatory Bodies:** Setting global AI standards.
- **Academia and Research Institutes:** Pushing the boundaries of AI innovation.
- **Businesses and Tech Giants:** Driving real-world AI applications at scale.

Quick Tip:

Join **AI consortiums** and **global partnerships** to stay ahead in the AI ecosystem.

Final Reflections: The Next Chapter is Yours

As we close this book, the next chapter belongs to **you, the reader**.

AI adoption isn't a finite journey—it's an ongoing evolution. The decisions you make today will shape the AI landscape of tomorrow.

Key Takeaways:

- AI success relies on **visionary leadership** and **practical execution**.
- Every organization must prioritize **ethical AI practices** and **governance frameworks**.
- Continuous learning, resilience, and collaboration will define long-term success.

Reflection Questions to Guide Your AI Strategy

- Are you investing enough in building AI talent and skills?
- Is your AI roadmap aligned with your long-term business vision?
- Are you prepared for the ethical, technical, and regulatory challenges of AI adoption?
- Are you measuring the right AI success metrics?

A Final Word: The Future is Now

The AI revolution isn't coming—it's already here.

Every line of code, every decision, and every insight generated by AI will shape industries, societies, and our collective future.

As leaders, innovators, and change-makers, your responsibility isn't just to adopt AI—it's to **shape it responsibly, ethically, and boldly.**

As you turn this final page, remember:

- Stay informed.
- Stay ethical.
- Stay adaptable.

Because the **AI journey doesn't end here—it begins with you.**

Let's lead, innovate, and build a better AI-powered world together. 🚀

- **Next Steps for Readers:**
- Revisit the chapters and align key insights with your AI strategy.
- Start your next AI pilot project with confidence.
- Share your learnings and collaborate with peers in the AI community.

Thank you for being part of this journey. The future is AI, and the future is now.

10

Bibliography

BOOKS AND REPORTS

1. **Russell, S., & Norvig, P.**(2020). Artificial Intelligence: A Modern Approach (4th Edition). Pearson Education.
2. A foundational text on AI concepts, algorithms, and real-world applications.
3. **Goodfellow, I., Bengio, Y., & Courville, A.**(2016). Deep Learning. MIT Press.
4. A comprehensive guide to the fundamentals and advancements in deep learning.
5. **Bostrom, N.**(2014). Superintelligence: Paths, Dangers, Strategies. Oxford University Press.
6. An exploration of the future implications of AI development.
7. **Brynjolfsson, E., & McAfee, A.**(2014). The Second Machine Age: Work, Progress, and Prosperity in a Time of Brilliant Technologies. W.W. Norton & Company.
8. A business-oriented perspective on the impact of AI and digital transformation.
9. **Chui, M., Manyika, J., & Miremadi, M.**(2018). Notes from the AI Frontier: Insights on the Economics

of Machine Learning and AI. McKinsey Global Institute.

10. A report on AI's economic impact, adoption strategies, and challenges.
11. **Articles and White Papers**
12. **OpenAI.**(2023). ChatGPT: Optimizing Language Models for Dialogue. OpenAI Blog. Retrieved from https://openai.com/blog/chatgpt.
13. **IBM Institute for Business Value.**(2021). The Enterprise Guide to AI Adoption. Retrieved from https://www.ibm.com.
14. **Gartner.**(2023). Top Strategic Technology Trends for 2024. Gartner Research. Retrieved from https://www.gartner.com.
15. **Online Resources**
16. **Statista.**(2023). Global Artificial Intelligence Market Size 2023-2030. Retrieved from https://www.statista.com.
17. **World Economic Forum.**(2022). Future of Jobs Report. Retrieved from https://www.weforum.org.
18. **Google AI.**(2023). Explainable AI (XAI): Tools and Techniques. Retrieved from https://ai.google/research.
19. **Case Studies and Real-World Examples**
20. **Amazon Web Services (AWS).**(2023). Scaling AI in Retail: A Case Study on Personalization with AWS ML Services. Retrieved from https://aws.amazon.com.
21. **Microsoft Azure.**(2022). AI-Powered Fraud Detection for Banking: A Case Study. Retrieved from https://azure.microsoft.com.
22. **Accenture.**(2021). AI for Cybersecurity: Building Resilience Against Threats. Retrieved from https://www.accenture.com.
23. **Additional References**
24. **European Commission.**(2023). AI Regulation and Ethical Guidelines. Retrieved from https://ec.europa.eu.

25. **National Institute of Standards and Technology (NIST).**(2022). AI Risk Management Framework. Retrieved from https://www.nist.gov.
26. **Harvard Business Review.**(2023). The Business Case for Ethical AI. Retrieved from https://hbr.org.
27. Fathima, N. (2024). The Intersection of Data Science and Ethics: Navigating Privacy and Bias. https://www.linkedin.com/pulse/intersection-data-science-ethics-navigating-privacy-bias-fathima-nb7qc
28. Klipfolio. (2024). What is a KPI Dashboard? Dashboard Examples & Best Practices. https://www.klipfolio.com/resources/dashboard-examples/executive/kpi-dashboard
29. McKinsey's. (2024). The state of AI in early 2024 | McKinsey. https://www.mckinsey.com/capabilities/quantumblack/our-insights/the-state-of-ai
30. RiseUp. (2021). Data Readiness | Rise Up Strategies. https://riseupstrategies.com/resources/data-readiness/
31. Shahriar, S., Allana, S., Hazratifard, S. M., & Dara, R. (2023). A Survey of Privacy Risks and Mitigation Strategies in the Artificial Intelligence Life Cycle. IEEE Access. https://doi.org/10.1109/ACCESS.2023.3287195
32. Visions, S. (2024). The AI Revolution: The Surge of AI Adoption Across Industries. Semantic Visions. https://www.semantic-visions.com/insights/ai-across-industries/

www.ingramcontent.com/pod-product-compliance
Lightning Source LLC
LaVergne TN
LVHW050408160826
845677LV00002BA/296

9798896915638